CLASSICS IN EDUCATION
Lawrence A. Cremin, General Editor

☆ ☆ ☆

THE REPUBLIC AND THE SCHOOL
Horace Mann on the Education of Free Men
Edited by Lawrence A. Cremin

AMERICAN IDEAS ABOUT ADULT EDUCATION
1710–1951
Edited by C. Hartley Grattan

DEWEY ON EDUCATION
Introduction and Notes by Martin S. Dworkin

THE SUPREME COURT AND EDUCATION
Edited by David Fellman

INTERNATIONAL EDUCATION
A Documentary History
Edited by David G. Scanlon

CRUSADE AGAINST IGNORANCE
Thomas Jefferson on Education
Edited by Gordon C. Lee

CHINESE EDUCATION UNDER COMMUNISM
Edited by Chang-Tu Hu

CHARLES W. ELIOT AND POPULAR EDUCATION
Edited by Edward A. Krug

VITTORINO DA FELTRE
AND OTHER HUMANIST EDUCATORS
By William Harrison Woodward
Foreword by Eugene F. Rice, Jr.

DESIDERIUS ERASMUS
CONCERNING THE AIM AND METHOD
OF EDUCATION
By William Harrison Woodward
Foreword by Craig R. Thompson

JOHN LOCKE ON EDUCATION
Edited by Peter Gay

CATHOLIC EDUCATION IN AMERICA
Edited by Neil G. McCluskey, S.J.

THE AGE OF THE ACADEMIES
Edited by Theodore R. Sizer

The Age
of the Academies

Edited, with an Introduction and Notes, by
THEODORE R. SIZER

CLASSICS IN

No. 22

EDUCATION

BUREAU OF PUBLICATIONS
TEACHERS COLLEGE, COLUMBIA UNIVERSITY
NEW YORK

Library of Congress Catalog Card
Number 64–24230

The illustration on the cover of the paperbound edition and on the jacket of the clothbound edition is a view of Lebanon, Connecticut, in 1835, showing Master Tisdale's school, an early academy, on the right. At the center is the meetinghouse designed by Colonel John Trumbull. One of the houses on the left was the residence of Jonathan Trumbull, governor of Connecticut. The wood block symbolizes well the early close association of school, state, and church. It was made by John Warner Barber and served as an illustration in his *Connecticut Historical Collections* . . . (New Haven, Conn., 1838), p. 319. The electrotype of the original is in the possession of the Yale University Art Gallery.

Printed in the United States of America
by the William Byrd Press, Inc.
Richmond, Virginia

Preface

"Most of the studies of the academy movement were written in the first years of this century," Dean Sizer points out, "and the neglect and distortion of the history of academies dates from that time." The most significant of the studies he is alluding to, of course, is Elmer Ellsworth Brown's *The Making of Our Middle Schools,* first published in 1903 and still the sole extant effort at a general history of American secondary education. Of twenty chapters, Brown gave five to the rise and fall of the academy, stressing the intellectual influence of Defoe and Milton in England and Franklin in the colonies, the key role of the Phillips academies as prototype institutions, the early effort to incorporate academies into statewide systems of education, and the general relation of the academy movement to the rise of the middle class. But on the whole, Brown viewed the movement as merely one aspect of "the age of transition from the partially stratified colonial society to modern democracy." Once the spokesmen for nineteenth-century democracy discovered that the academy was not truly susceptible to public control, the academy passed, and the more "democratic" high school took its place.

In contrast, Dean Sizer's effort is to study "the uniqueness and significance of the academy movement irrespective of its effect on the development of public education." He is thereby able to portray the academy as a characteristic institution of ante-bellum America. Its organizational structure, emphasizing control by a board of prominent citizens who often held a charter from a state legislature, closely paralleled that of other quasi-public enterprises such as banks, canals, and colleges. Its curriculum, addressed to the needs of ambitious entrepreneurs (Marvin Meyers has called them "venturous conservatives"), reflected a typical Jacksonian optimism about class mobility. And its novelty and flexibility, coupled with a laissez-faire attitude on the part of state governments, permitted its adaptation to a wide variety of specific purposes and local circumstances.

Equally important, perhaps, Dean Sizer's approach enables him to view the passing of the academies, not as the triumph of democracy over elitism, but rather as one aspect of post-Civil War urbanization. "The academy failed because it was fundamentally a rural institution," he concludes, "a school uniquely appropriate for a population thinly spread." In the burgeoning cities of industrial America, it was the day high school that flourished, largely as an upward extension of elementary education. The academies, mostly boarding schools, became uneconomical, and those that wanted to survive were forced to transform themselves more than ever into special-purpose institutions. To see the development thus is not merely to remove the stigma of elitism from the early academies (a stigma first imposed, incidentally, by Horace Mann and other public school reformers); it is to open the way to a fuller understanding of their crucial significance in the popularization of American education.

LAWRENCE A. CREMIN

Contents

The Age
of the Academies

The Academies: An Interpretation

By THEODORE R. SIZER

Few social institutions in American history better exemplify the grand optimism of the people of this republic than do the academies. These schools, roughly described as those providing instruction beyond rudimentary literacy and computation, were the outgrowth of enthusiasm for formal education on the part of local leaders, philanthropists, state legislatures, and the people at large. While many have long since vanished, in their day these academies, founded locally or regionally, flourished and in a small way provided the country as a whole with what is now called secondary education. The age of the academies, that is, the period of their greatest development, extended roughly from the Revolution to the Civil War and was an era well known for its grand, unrealistic optimism in the power of institutions to perfect man. Thousands of academies of one type or another sprang up during these eight decades; one observer counted six thousand in 1850, but he was probably conservative in his estimate.[1] Their impact on American cultural life must have been considerable. And the fact that they were founded and supported, often at great sacrifice, is important for an understanding of the towns and counties of ante-bellum America.

[1] Henry Barnard, "Educational Statistics of the United States in 1850," *American Journal of Education,* I (1855), 368.

Although there was a bewildering variety of academies, two characteristics distinguish them. They can be isolated from other institutions on the basis of their administrative structure, their relatively private form of control. They can also be defined by their curriculum, which was broader and more "practical" than that of their predecessor, the Latin grammar school. Although there were important exceptions, most academies incorporated both these features.[2]

Most academies were private or, at most, quasi-public schools. By "private" is meant that the control of policy was in the hands of a board of self-perpetuating or otherwise relatively independent trustees. Most academies were *not* private in the sense that they received no local, state, or federal money toward their support; in fact, funds from the public purse constituted a major, indeed crucial, element in the financing of the schools. Most academies were *not* private in the sense that they limited enrollment to particular groups within the society; the majority were open to all in the sense that the public schools of England are "open." Indeed, most implored all comers to enroll, bearing their life-giving tuition. Some of the academies, independently controlled, were treated as local schools and provided education on an unrestricted basis for all the children of the community who had the desire and the wherewithal to attend.

It is well to remember that the small, often state-

[2] As a result, few historians have bothered to treat these characteristics independently. Many found the academy "private" and thus *ipso facto* an unhappy restraint on the growth of the public high school. This interpretation of the academies as an undemocratic throwback to European elitism overlooks the grass-roots support for these establishments and casts the academy movement in a thoroughly misleading light. Bernard Bailyn has discussed the biases of these "public school" historians in *Education in the Forming of American Society* (Chapel Hill, N.C., 1960).

chartered, "private" corporation was a common institution in ante-bellum America. At the heart of the Jacksonian movement was the small businessman, the "village
entrepreneur." And while few individuals or localities
founded academies as business enterprises, their institutions did resemble the burgeoning small manufactories of
the time in administrative structure. The founders were
ambitious in their plans, organizing the academies as
relatively independent institutions, usually tied closely
to the local community. They often acquired for them
charters from the state legislatures, charters which themselves, due to a series of important court cases starting in
1819 with the famous Dartmouth College case, gave protection from the state, at the same time making it possible, in many instances, for these institutions to acquire
state aid. The "private" institutional form was utterly
characteristic of the time and had long been the pattern
of collegiate organization; that the academies took this
form should be no surprise. Indeed, when they took other
forms, particularly a wholly public form, locally or state
operated, they languished.[3]

The Latin grammar school, which preceded the academy as the principal bridge between common school and
college, had been organized and controlled in a somewhat
different manner. The Latin schools of New England
were town schools, governed by an elected group and
supported by local and, often, state grants. They were,
in fact, more like twentieth-century public schools than
were the nineteenth-century academies that succeeded

[3] An illuminating statement on this public-private issue is Theodore Edson, "On the Comparative Merits of Private and Public
Schools," in American Institute of Instruction, *Proceedings, 1837*, pp.
93–107. Edson concluded that the public schools were "vigorous
branches of education," and the private schools, "its fanciful, and
oftentimes beautiful excrescences" (p. 106).

them. They were founded, however, only in areas where
the population was dense enough to support them ("100
families," the Massachusetts Law of 1647 stipulated);
and the rural areas were left without institutions of
formal education beyond the district schools, if that. In
addition, there were the small, ephemeral, private-
venture schools which sprang up for specialized and,
most often, practical purposes in the towns of the East.
These, providing courses in modern languages or bookkeeping or English or navigation, were usually one-man
enterprises; the school was the teacher, and as long as he
could make ends meet, the school remained open. These
shadowy enterprises, whose existence remains for us in
many cases only in newspaper advertisements and printed
broadsides, were limited in their purpose and were as
"private" as the Colonial Latin school had been "public."
Both languished or, to put it more accurately, were
absorbed in spirit by the academy. Their institutional
framework was exchanged for the more timely, relatively
private form previously mentioned.

The successor of the academy, in one sense, was the
public high school. Institutionally, this school was but an
appendage of the locally controlled and supported common school, the public nature of which had been fully
re-established by the legislatures of most states during
the Jacksonian period and the decades following. The
high school was controlled in the same fashion as the
common schools, that is, by an elected body of local
citizens. It was neither a private nor a quasi-public venture, but a completely public institution. It looked more
like the Latin school than the academy in this important
respect. The age of the academies lay between the periods
in which these two similar institutional forms—the
"public" Latin school and the public high school—

flourished and was marked by relatively more private endeavor.

The academy, then, can be characterized in one way as an institution "privately" controlled, often chartered, with close local and state ties in terms of both student body and financial support. A second way of defining the institution is by its purpose, as reflected in its curriculum. It is here that the grand optimism of the academy found-ers is so apparent. How lofty was the rationale for the Phillips Academy at Andover: "to learn [the students] the great end and real business of living"! Almost a century after Andover's founding, an academy in Ver-mont was still making the same claim: its most important purpose was "to furnish the youth of [this] vicinity . . . the means of securing a sound, practical education, for the business of life."[4] Iowa's first academy called for "the instruction of young persons of both sexes in science and literature."[5] The same idea and even the same words—business of life, science, literature—were repeated over and over again in foundations in every part of the country. These statements reveal not only a great faith in the power of formal schooling to prepare boys and girls for "life" but also an assumption that "life" was in many respects a here-and-now matter, for which one prepared by studies of a here-and-now nature, by subjects "use-ful" as well as "ornamental," as Benjamin Franklin put it. The program of the academy represented a break from the medieval curriculum of the Latin school. There was more in this "preparation for life" than simply Latin, Greek, and arithmetic; there were English, the modern

---

[4] Catalogue of the Barre (Vermont) Academy (Barre, Vt., 1852), n.p.

[5] Clarence R. Aurner, *History of Education in Iowa* (Iowa City, Iowa, 1914–1920), III, 3.

languages, algebra, history, and the practical arts of
navigation, agriculture, surveying, and pedagogy. The
academy, then, can be defined as an institution that departed somewhat from the narrow classical tradition
represented by the Latin school. While it most often
retained the classical studies of its forebear, it added to
them the more practical subjects offered by the Colonial
private-venture schools.

Needless to say, the American academy was not the first
formal educational institution to break from the earlier
mold. It had many predecessors, but it is often difficult
to trace their influence precisely. The impact of John
Milton's educational plan on the early development of
the American academy, however, can be seen rather
clearly; his essay *Of Education* is cited throughout Franklin's proposals, and it found its way into numerous educational journals during the nineteenth century.[6] In *Of
Education,* Milton attacks the dull classics instruction
in seventeenth-century England and then goes on to describe the form of an academy. His proposed curriculum
is broad, although many of his "practical" courses comprise study of the classics: agriculture is to be learned
from Cato and Varro, and law from Moses, Licurgus, and
others. Milton is protesting not against the wisdom of
the ancients but against the abuse of their writings by
rote study and busy work, the "too oft idle vacancies
given both to Schools and Universities." Milton sees his
academy as more than a school for linguistic training. It

[6] The *American Journal of Education,* for example, printed the
Tractate at least three times: II (1856), 76; XXII (1871), 181;
XXIII (1872), 151. It should be stressed that the term "academy" was applied to many kinds of institutions by Milton and
countless others before and after. It has been so indiscriminately
used that in itself it gives no clue as to the kind of educational
institution it signifies.

is to provide practical schooling, even taking responsibility for the students' physical health.

There was opportunity for Milton's plan to find its
way into practice, for with the Restoration and the re-
strictive acts of 1662, Puritan teaching was driven from
the established and endowed schools and universities,
and teachers were required to take an oath of loyalty to
the Church of England. Largely in response to the closing
of Oxford and Cambridge to non-Anglicans, dissenting
groups organized their own institutions, which they
called, presumably after Milton, academies. Their curricula paralleled those of the classical grammar schools
and universities but included, in the pattern suggested
by Milton, more practical subjects as well, subjects
such as navigation, English, and the modern languages, which were useful in the business world in which
many wealthy dissenters were finding fortunes. The English, or dissenting, academies were essentially schools of
religious protest, but they were also a reaction against
the narrow curriculum so entrenched in the schools and
universities of the time.[7]

It is no surprise that these particular institutions found
Benjamin Franklin an admirer. While Franklin would
hardly have been sympathetic to Milton's belief that
"the end . . . of Learning is to repair the ruines of our
first Parents," he did find happy that Puritan's plan
for a school with a bias more practical than that of the
Latin school, a school which over the years in England
had established a reputation for being suited to those em-
barking on careers in commerce.[8] Franklin himself was

[7] See Irene Parker, *Dissenting Academies in England* (Cambridge,
England, 1914).

[8] See John J. O'Neill, "An Analysis of Franklin's Proposals . . ."
(Unpublished doctoral dissertation, Harvard University, 1960). See

the product of no institutional system. His education had
been informal, but effective indeed, and he retained a
clear bias toward such informal self-education; his Junto,
the forerunner of the American Philosophical Society, is
evidence enough of that. Deploring existing educational
institutions in America, Franklin suggested a reform—
the establishment of an academy with a curriculum
broader than that of the classical grammar school.[9] Always a good politician, he possibly saw that his conservative readers would oppose his ideas; and in printing
them, he literally engulfed his text in footnotes from
indisputably reputable English sources, most notably,
the writings of Milton and Locke. Thus did he hope to
win supporters for his academy.

Franklin's plan finally evolved into the "college,
Academy, and charitable School of Philadelphia," the
course of study of which was divided into two parts, a
classical curriculum in the traditional Latin-school mold
and an English curriculum somewhat like that suggested
in his academy plan. From the start the latter suffered
at the hands of the first provost, William Smith, and
Franklin's protests were of no avail.[10] The grand scheme
to teach the "most useful and most ornamental" failed,

---

also John Hardin Best, ed., *Benjamin Franklin on Education* (New
York, 1962), a companion volume in the present series, and Robert
Middlekauff, *Ancients and Axioms: Secondary Education in Eight-
eenth-Century New England* (New Haven, Conn., 1963), Chapter 8.

[9] As "Silence Dogood" in his brother's newspaper, Franklin, at
the age of sixteen, cast his barbs at exalted Harvard, to which he
referred caustically as "the Temple of Learning." Harvard students,
he asserted, were "great Blockheads," both before and after their
sojourn in Cambridge. See Samuel Eliot Morison, *Three Centuries
of Harvard, 1636–1936* (Cambridge, Mass., 1936), p. 61.

[10] Franklin published his *Idea of the English School* in 1751,
presumably to give some life to his scheme for useful studies. The
text can be found in Robert Ulich, *Three Thousand Years of Edu-*

and Franklin's academy eventually became what we know today as the University of Pennsylvania.

While Franklin's own academy could not sustain the sort of curriculum reform and expansion that he had proposed, the idea of a course of study wider and more useful than that of the Latin school increased in influence. The narrow classical curriculum was simply out of step with the ideas of the this-worldly, commercial, optimistic American, who often associated traditional learning with the social distinctions he wished America to avoid. There was, in a word, disjunction between the expectations of society and the offerings of the Latin schools,[11] and in the few areas of the country where they had been established, largely in the Northeast, they declined in number and influence. Americans were interested in supporting studies, if not wholly vocational in the modern sense, at least useful in Franklin's sense. The academies, which provided both the classics and the more modern subjects, met their desires.

While the distinction between the Latin school and the academy on the basis of the curriculum is quite clear, that between the academy and its "successor," the high school, is not. The public high school, being the product of the grading and upward expansion of the common school, not surprisingly offered advanced work in the subjects of the primary school; its curriculum, as

---

cational Wisdom (Cambridge, Mass., 1954), pp. 448–453, or in Best, ed., *Benjamin Franklin on Education*, pp. 165–171.

[11] The notion of disjunction is spelled out well, if for a later period, in Oscar Handlin, *John Dewey's Challenge to Education* (New York, 1959). On the Latin schools, see Middlekauff, *Ancients and Axioms,* especially Chapter 9, and Mary A. Connolly, "Boston Schools in the New Republic" (Unpublished doctoral dissertation, Harvard University, 1963). Middlekauff sees financial distress as the prime cause of the Latin school's decline in New England.

one high-school principal argued, was "practically the systematic expansion . . . of the modern studies mapped out for the elementary schools."[12] Thus, the modern studies—English, mathematics, history, and the others— were found in the high school, there joined by Latin and, less often, Greek. The curriculum of the high school was quite similar to that of the academy, then, the only real difference being that the former institution borrowed few of the unusual or vocational subjects found in the latter, subjects such as pedagogy, psychology, and agriculture. The high school tended to narrow its offerings to Latin and the principal modern studies of the lower grades. The academy separated it in time from the Latin school, with its narrow, heavily linguistic course of study, consisting of Latin, Greek, and arithmetic. Thus, the academy can be defined as an institution with a curriculum more closely attuned to the wants of nineteenth-century America than that of its predecessor and one in which every conceivable subject of possible intellectual or practical value was offered.

Having defined academies in two ways—on the basis of both their institutional form and their curriculum— it should be said that while most academies fit both definitions (i.e., they were "private" or quasi-public institutions offering instruction in both the classical studies and the more useful and modern subjects), there were important exceptions. Governor Dummer Academy, for example, being a privately chartered school, met the first criterion and is often labeled the "first" academy in New England; but its curriculum was clearly traditional. "Dummer School," wrote an observer during the Civil War, "under the administration of Master Moody [the

12 R. G. Huling, in New England Association of Colleges and Preparatory Schools, *Addresses and Proceedings, 1894,* p. 5.

first teacher], was the best type of an English [Latin] grammar school that had existed on American soil since the days of Ezekiel Cheever."[13] Its feeble efforts at physical training and instruction in the modern languages hardly made it an academy in the sense of our second definition. Other New England academies were essentially country boarding schools with Latin grammar curricula, which were broadened only slightly in the early days. The English Classical School, founded in Boston in 1821, exemplifies a second class of exceptions. Now called the English High School (the "English" to contrast with the ancient Boston Latin School), this institution had a course of study including English, geography, arithmetic, algebra, geometry, trigonometry, history, navigation, and surveying, clearly the curriculum of an academy, as we have defined it. The Classical School was, however, a wholly public institution, governed by the School Committee of the City of Boston and supported largely by public moneys. Here, then, we have an institution that was not an academy by virtue of its "private" or quasi-public administrative structure, but clearly an academy on the basis of its curriculum and the intent of its founders. Boston found the "public" tradition comfortable, and its academy, resulting from the same kinds of pressures that led to the creation of other institutions offering modern studies, took the form of a public school.

The academy movement, then, is not easy to label, but the general pattern—the establishment of schools offering a wide variety of subjects beyond the rudiments and organized largely on a private basis—is clearly apparent, the several exceptions notwithstanding.

[13] Charles Hammond, "New England Academies and Classical Schools, *American Journal of Education*, XVI (1866), 410.

II

Largely as a result of the paucity of records and the vary-
ing interpretations of just what an academy was, it is
less clear exactly how many such schools existed in America
during the nineteenth century. In 1855, Henry Barnard
made a careful study, cataloguing three kinds of institutions: colleges, academies, and public schools. He located
239 of the first and 80,978 of the last. Of academies, he
counted 6,185, in which a total of 263,096 pupils were
enrolled; the colleges, he found, enrolled 27,821. In each
of five states, he reported, over 10,000 students attended
academies: in New York, 49,328; in Pennsylvania, 23,751;
in Ohio, 15,052; in Massachusetts, 13,436; and in Kentucky, 12,712. New York had 887 separate institutions,
more than any other state.[14]

Other scholars have arrived at different figures. Alexander Inglis identified only 135 incorporated academies
in Massachusetts in 1850 compared with Barnard's 403,
but he also found hundreds of unincorporated and what
he termed "private" academies, 640 by 1859–1860.[15]
Walter Gifford located 286 academies chartered in New
York by 1850 and estimated that about one-half were
actually operating in that year.[16] While Barnard's figures
include both incorporated and unincorporated institutions and are thus higher than those of many others, the
fact remains that even if one takes the most conservative
estimate—and even Barnard's may be conservative, considering the probable high number of ephemeral acad-

[14] Barnard, in the *American Journal of Education*, I (1855), 368.
[15] Alexander J. Inglis, *The Rise of the High School in Massachusetts* (New York, 1911), pp. 8, 57.
[16] Walter J. Gifford, *Historical Development of the New York
State High School System* (Albany, N.Y., 1922), pp. 187–188.

emies that were known only locally and for which no records remain—one is impressed by two phenomena: the large number of academies founded and the national spread of these institutions. Many Americans attended them, by Barnard's count for 1850, fully nine times as many as went to the colleges. And these essentially private institutions, the outgrowth of local enterprise particularly, were found in every state and territory of the United States. Even raw Texas had 97 academies by 1850.[17]

The important question is, of course, why this grass-roots, unorganized, but national growth of academies took place. The spontaneity of the expansion implies the existence of common patterns of belief among leaders, even small-town leaders, across the country as a whole. These patterns are complex.

"The business of education has acquired a new complexion by the independence of our country," wrote Benjamin Rush in 1798. He called for teaching of both republican duties and republican principles in the schools: "Let our pupil be taught that he does not belong to himself, but that he is public property." Rush concluded simply that "it is possible to convert men into republican machines."[18] And the schools were to be the agents of conversion, the means of assuring the permanence of the American form of government. An educated electorate was the cornerstone of democracy, and democratic government had to provide for it. These sentiments played a particularly important role in the struggle for common schools, for the teaching of rudimentary lit-

[17] Barnard, in the *American Journal of Education*, I (1855), 368.
[18] Benjamin Rush, "Of the Mode of Education Proper in a Republic," in Dagobert D. Runes, ed., *The Selected Writings of Benjamin Rush* (New York, 1947), pp. 87, 90, 92.

eracy and computation that the unsophisticated American felt to be sufficient to prepare an intelligent voter. Yet they influenced the growth of academies and colleges as well; the early leaders, Rush among them, constructed on paper elaborate educational systems, all of which were crowned by institutions to train a talented elite, the men who would lead the nation.

Jefferson's system is probably the best known; he called for schools of secondary grade as well as a university. Virginia failed to follow its greatest leader's plan, however, and only gave him late in his life the consolation of the University of Virginia.[19] Similar schemes for an educational pyramid including schools of secondary grade were outlined in several early state constitutions, and the implementation of these was seen as a clear public responsibility. Unfortunately, however, these hopeful plans foundered, as had Jefferson's, the victims both of less radical, laissez-faire politicians and of economic difficulties. The republican argument for schooling beyond the rudiments remained, however, and served as a spur to men in Jackson's time who were eager for the erection of educational systems. "In the United States politics are the end and aim of education," wrote Alexis de Tocqueville in the 1830's.[20] This belief surely encouraged the republican-minded Americans to erect schools for the benefit of their fledgling democracy. "The permanence of our institutions, must depend upon the intelligence of the great mass of the people," argued Iowa's Governor Dodge in 1836; and his legislature went

[19] See Gordon C. Lee, ed., *Crusade Against Ignorance: Thomas Jefferson on Education* (New York, 1961), an earlier volume in this series.

[20] Alexis de Tocqueville, *Democracy in America,* translated by Henry Reeve (Galaxy ed.; New York, 1947), p. 208.

on to incorporate that state's first academy.[21] The case for republicanism's dependence on formal schooling has rarely been argued more succinctly than in the Connecticut school law of 1799: children "shall be instructed in such course and order as to give all an equal opportunity."[22]

Associated with this interest in the schools as the manufacturers of "republican machines" was the assumption that schools do teach and that formal education is a desirable part of life. This is in a sense paradoxical: the unintellectual American so despised by Mrs. Trollope and other genteel European visitors had a reverence for book learning. The explanation of the paradox may rest on the fact that Americans built academies for useful studies rather than universities, lyceums rather than cultivated salons. De Tocqueville recognized this phenomenon: "I do not believe that there is a country in the world where, in proportion to the population, there are so few uninstructed and at the same time so few learned individuals."[23] The academy fit the American ideal: it provided a smattering of both useful studies and traditional book learning, a veneer of education. This was considered good by Americans who distrusted the narrow erudition of the college graduate. Americans were hopeful that some learning of a practical kind might better them, might help them become, as George Orwell more recently put it, "more equal." There was no profound love of learning for its own sake, no intellectual aspiration here.

[21] As quoted in Aurner, *History of Education in Iowa,* III, 3.
[22] As quoted in Harvey S. Reed, "The Period of the Academy in Connecticut" (Unpublished doctoral dissertation, Yale University, 1942), p. 52.
[23] De Tocqueville, *Democracy in America,* p. 44. A thorough study of this paradox is provided in Richard Hofstadter's *Anti-intellectualism in American Life* (New York, 1963), Chapters 2, 10, 12.

There was the material hope of getting ahead and the political hope of improving the republic. The academy founder was the optimistic entrepreneur rather than the reflective scholar.

While this optimistic faith in education affected the growth of academies, it influenced the common-school and college movements as well. The republican argument—and the fear on the part of the conservative members of the community of an illiterate and therefore unconservative mob—carried particular weight in the struggle to erect public primary schools in all parts of the country. In some areas, however, particularly in the South, the "private" academies were often competitors to the common schools. A small, cheaply run academy which, despite pretensions, offered training in the rudiments could salve the consciences and protect the purses of the local people and at the same time provide for the few children who wanted to go to school at least the semblance of an education. By the Civil War, however, the disadvantages of this catch-as-catch-can system had become obvious, and several states, most notably those in New England and the Middle West, were erecting common-school systems which were public, in the present sense of the word.[24]

The pressures that sparked the prodigious growth of the colleges were similar to those that spurred the academy movement. Frederick Rudolph has characterized them nicely:

College-founding in the nineteenth century was undertaken in the same spirit as canal-building, cotton-ginning, farming, and gold-mining. In none of these activities did completely rational procedures prevail. All were touched by the American faith in

[24] See Lawrence A. Cremin, *The American Common School: An Historic Conception* (New York, 1951).

tomorrow, in the unquestionable capacity of Americans to achieve a better world. In the founding of colleges, reason could not combat the romantic belief in endless progress.[25]

Added to this was the religious zeal of the denominations and the pride of states and localities. Methodists, Presbyterians, Baptists, Congregationalists, Roman Catholics, and others all struggled to build institutions to promote their particular persuasions, not only in the settled East, but especially in the newly opened lands of the Middle West. They worked in a time of religious enthusiasm, and many of the hilltop colleges of today trace their origins to the ante-bellum sectarian competition. Local and state groups, eager to add lustre to their new and struggling communities and to attract additional and, hopefully, desirable settlers and investors, actively sought the colleges, often with little regard for any particular religious denomination. The legislatures chartered colleges of all descriptions and tried in almost every instance to found state universities to cap the educational systems that the more radical of them visualized.[26] With those attempting to erect common-school systems and academies, then, the college founders exhibited a trusting belief in formal education. It was good for the republic, and it was good for the individual, perfectible as he was.

The academies, however, grew in far greater numbers than did the colleges. The reasons for this are obvious. The college, particularly when it tried to maintain the

[25] Frederick Rudolph, *The American College and University: A History* (New York, 1962), pp. 48–49.

[26] America had nine colleges by the beginning of the Revolution and about 250 at the time of the Civil War. Several hundred additional institutions had been established during the period but had failed. This wave of college-founding was unique to nineteenth-century America. See Rudolph, *The American College and University*, p. 47.

legacy of conservative Yale and Princeton, smacked of aristocracy and had a difficult task all through the Jacksonian years in justifying its curriculum to the public. The academy offered a more flexible and useful course of study and became a strong competitor to the college, for most fledgling colleges were taking students as young and as untutored as were the academies.[27] The extent of the competition to the colleges is most clearly seen in the famous report of the faculty of Yale in 1828, in which President Jeremiah Day and his associates eloquently justified the narrow classical curriculum at Yale. Academies are specifically, if politely, attacked in the text:

Why [should the college] wish to take [the academies' and similar institutions'] business out of their hands? The college has its appropriate object, and they have theirs. . . . What is the characteristic difference between a college and an academy? Not that the former teaches more branches than the latter. There are many academies in the country, whose scheme of studies, at least upon paper, is more various than that of the colleges. But while an academy teaches a little of every thing, the college, by directing its efforts to one uniform course, aims at doing its work with greater precision, and economy of time; just as the merchant who deals in a single class of commodities, or a manufacturer who produces but one kind of fabrics, executes his business more perfectly, than he whose attention and skill are divided among a multitude of objects.[28]

27 Which, of course, raises another question of definition: When was a college a college and not an academy? The overlap between the two was still so great in some states in the 1890's that for statistical purposes they were lumped together in state reports. In 1850, however, Barnard felt he could make some kind of distinction, largely, one might guess, on the basis of curriculum.

28 "Original Papers in Relation to a Course of Liberal Education," *The American Journal of Science and the Arts,* XV (1829), 318–319. One would guess that Day and his colleagues were concerned as well over the potential harm that the new University of Virginia, with its novel design, might render to academic standards.

The American, however, then and since, seemed to prefer that the "multitude" be superficially accomplished rather than the single class exquisitely perfected. The offerings of the college were simply too limited to appeal to any great number of Americans. The events in higher education after the Civil War would demonstrate this even more fully.

Preferred were the more utilitarian institutions like the academy, the lyceum, and the library. The lyceums, springing up in considerable numbers during the 1830's, were local groups that banded together for self-improvement, one member teaching his skill to the next. Lyceums collected "cabinets" of scientific specimens and undertook worthy causes, including the establishment of common schools and academies.[29] Their belief in the possibility of mutual improvement was too optimistic, however; and their meetinghouses rapidly became the way stations on important lecture circuits, over which such intellectually influential men as Alexander Agassiz, Edward Everett, Oliver Wendell Holmes, Henry David Thoreau, and Ralph Waldo Emerson rode in pre-Civil War days. The public libraries were testimony to the same belief in self-education of a this-worldly, practical sort. The academies, of course, reflected this optimism and wedded it institutionally to the symbolically respectable classical curriculum of Latin and mathematics. The academy was the American's compromise between practical education and the education traditionally held valuable.

It is clear that denominational squabbling was far less a cause for the growth of academies than it was for

[29] See Josiah Holbrook, "The American Lyceum, or Society for Improvement of Schools and Diffusion of Useful Knowledge," *American Journal of Education,* III (1828), 715–721.

the growth of colleges. Local communities needed schools of the lower grades far more than they needed colleges. As Barnard put it, in speaking of Massachusetts, "the needs of families not residing within towns [which had public Latin grammar schools] made obligatory by law, led to the establishment of a class of institutions known as Academies."[30] Far fewer sectarian than non-sectarian academies were founded in Vermont; the same was true in Mississippi.[31] Only about one-third of Indiana's academies were sectarian, the "most successful" Protestant group being the Quakers.[32] Considering that virtually all the colleges founded during the first half of the nineteenth century were primarily the outgrowth of sectarian zeal, the contrast is striking. The academy was clearly a product of local civic effort; it was not godless, to be sure, but while charged with the moral instruction of its students, it was clearly an institution designed essentially to serve the needs of this world. Of the five "purposes" of the Barre Academy in Vermont, two are quite specific—college preparation and teacher training; two are vaguely humanistic—"sound, practical education" for boys and "a liberal education" for girls; and only the last has a somewhat moral tone—"to promote virtue, morality, and piety in the young."[33] The

[30] Henry Barnard, "Incorporated Academies and Seminaries," *American Journal of Education,* XXX (1880), 761.

[31] Edward D. Andrews, *The County Grammar Schools and Academies of Vermont* (Brattleboro, Vt., 1936), pp. 177–180, and William H. Weatherby, *A History of Educational Legislation in Mississippi from 1798 to 1860* (Chicago, 1921), p. 74.

[32] Albert Mock, *The Mid-western Academy Movement* (Indianapolis, Ind., cop. 1949), pp. 24–29.

[33] Catalogue of the Barre (Vermont) Academy, n.p. Of course there were important exceptions. See Mother M. Benedict Murphy, "Pioneer Roman Catholic Girls' Academies . . ." (Unpublished doctoral dissertation, Columbia University, 1958).

same general pattern of priorities was revealed in the larger portion of the institutions. The majority were "nonsectarian," liberal Protestant establishments, in religious observance quite like the common schools of their day. Local pride and demand played a far more important role in the establishment of academies than anything else, and the common practice of assigning the name of the town to the academy—Barre Academy, for example—demonstrates the close tie between the institution and its community.

Why, then, it can be asked, did not the academy emerge as a publicly supported, completely popular institution? The answer is the same as that explaining the slowness of the growth of common schools: the American was *for* many things, but he was not for being heavily taxed. As long as the money did not come out of the individual's pocket, but rather from rents or interest on a literature fund, the towns and states supported academies and schools. When these indirect sources of finance proved too small, the public institutions withered.[34] But while the American was opposed to a general and continuing tax, he believed enough in education to dignify a private venture with a charter and to set it on its way with an initial grant of money or, more usually, of land. Assistance to the academies most often took the form of public encouragement and sporadic aid rather than continuing full financial support. Relative laissez faire seemed a reasonable policy for corporate business; it was applied as well to the academies and colleges.

The academies emerged in remarkable numbers in

[34] Reed, "The Period of the Academy in Connecticut," p. 52. There were, of course, important exceptions, such as the Norwich (Connecticut) Free Academy and the Boston English Classical School.

nineteenth-century America for this variety of reasons. Belief in equality and in the need of a republic for an educated citizenry, belief in practical education and in the perfectibility of man, local pride, the tendency to encourage private endeavor rather than continuing public responsibility—all had their impact. Thousands of institutions were the result.

III

It has been said that schools are the result of men and money. The academies owed their rapid growth to many of the former and their instability and often marginal quality to a lack of the latter.

Most often, academies were founded by groups of men who organized themselves into boards of trustees. Some drew on their own resources to get a school going or petitioned the state for a charter and an initial grant. Others set up a stock company, gathered small amounts of money for each share of stock, and permitted the shareholders to vote for the trustees. Rarely, however, was any dividend expected to accrue. Support for the academies was not usually offered from thought of gain; it was considered a duty.

The trustees' task was to find building, teacher, and students; all were difficult to locate. Seldom did an academy have its own building in its early years, and other expedients had to be arranged. Teachers were difficult to obtain, particularly good ones, and the turnover was high. Many reminiscences have come down to us, describing the tortuous ways in which boards of trustees attempted to examine a prospective teacher, quizzing him on his subjects and his morality. Students bearing the all-important tuition were not always easy to find, and the trustees used various devices for attracting them. By and large, the trustees played the major role in the control and operation of their schools. Local clergy were very active both on and off the boards of trustees. While there were exceptions like the doughty Eliphalet Pearson of Andover, the teachers were generally short-term hired hands with little power. Since the academies were mostly private ventures, the abilities of the boards were crucial. If they failed, the academies failed.

The critical factor was financial support, and the sponsors of academies used many devices to scrape it together. The most important source was tuition, which, although rarely high, was probably the easiest and surest means of keeping an academy running. Tuition was almost universally expected and was often assessed on the basis of the subjects taken, the classical languages, for example, costing more than the rudiments. The fees did not always come in the form of money, but often as goods, such as flour, wood, or even labor.

Next to the students, the state was probably the most important benefactor. As has been mentioned, several states themselves took the initiative in founding "secondary-school systems": Indiana and Iowa tried "county seminaries," Vermont "county grammar schools," and Michigan lower branches of the university in a number of towns away from Ann Arbor. Almost without exception, these "systems" failed; they were too ambitious and their public character premature. The states were *for* education, but they found that in the last analysis, support of private ventures was more congenial and less of a drag on the public purse.

Several states, however, gave considerable backing to the "private" academies and conceived of them as parts of a co-ordinated system, albeit a "privately" controlled one. Most states made grants of money or land to the institutions they chartered. Many had "literature funds," which were dispensed in support of common schools, academies, and colleges, although by the late 1830's, several states cut the colleges and the academies off the list and concentrated the meager amounts on the primary schools.[35] Each state handled the problem of educational support differently, and the generalizations one can make are few: all states exhibited concern over providing formal education beyond the rudiments, all aided by giving charters to private ventures, most used the proceeds from the sale of public land to aid education; but all failed until after the Civil War to create within their borders a genuine system of schools offering studies beyond the three R's.

Two states which were particularly active deserve a closer examination. In 1806, Tennessee received a Congressional grant of one hundred thousand acres of federal land within her borders, with the stipulation that the proceeds from the sale of this property should accrue to the state-sponsored county academies. The state agreed and set up an academy fund alongside a college and common-school fund. Despite the usual difficulties in selling the land, some academies opened nominally in 1807, their trustees being appointed by the legislature. But times were hard, and the income from the state insufficient; the academies, like so many of their cousins in other states, had to depend largely on local private support. In 1840, the Bank of Tennessee exchanged an assured annual grant of $18,000 to the academies for the fluctuating returns from the public land

[35] See, for example, Edgar W. Knight, *The Academy Movement in the South* (n.p. [Chapel Hill, N.C.], n.d. [1920]), p. 24; reprinted from *The High School Journal*, Vols. II–III (1919–1920).

funds. The county academies apparently benefited from this arrangement until the Civil War.[36] Tennessee is an example, then, of a state relatively active in the support of her academies. At the same time her experience demonstrates the ever-present need for local assistance and, by virtue of the loose form of government chosen to run the county academies (i.e., appointed trustees), the relaxed control over the state-sponsored education of the period.

New York furnishes another example of relatively active state involvement. A series of acts in the late eighteenth century established a Board of Regents to oversee education within the state. The Regents passed on the qualifications of academies for their incorporation and administered a fund for their support. What was novel about the New York arrangement was that the Regents tied strings to their money: they inspected academies, and they required regular reports. Although the aid they dispensed never represented the largest portion of the academies' income, it was sufficient to enable the schools to provide studies that the Regents desired.[37] Teacher education was the most significant of the Regents' requests, and the academies provided normal-school training for a large number of New York's common-school teachers. In so doing they delayed somewhat the development of separate normal schools in that state. The Regents also required the academies to provide college-preparatory studies. Thus did control follow support, at least in New York; her academies flourished in number and quality owing to the interest of the state and the

[36] Knight, *The Academy Movement in the South*, pp. 27 ff.

[37] In 1825, the state provided $6,220 to the $23,558 the academies raised through tuition; in 1850, the comparable figures were $40,000 and $237,051. See George F. Miller, *The Academy System of the State of New York* (Albany, N.Y., 1922), p. 76.

activity of the Board of Regents. The state, however, neither founded academies nor required towns to do so; it simply supported those which were established by private initiative. Large parts of the state were left without facilities, and the Regents never had full control: a board of trustees could ignore their strictures if it was willing to forego the state's financial aid, a policy many obviously preferred. New York's state control was loose indeed.[38]

While the students and the state provided the principal financial support for the academies, innumerable other sources were also tapped. A few academies were blessed with reasonably large endowments; many of these, such as the Phillips academies, have survived difficult financial times and exist today, their current endowments running in the tens of millions of dollars. But these remained the exceptions, since few of the thousands of institutions could count on any endowment at all. Gifts they received, but not enduring gifts: "one day's work, one horse collar, one steel trap, five pounds of coffee, six pounds of sugar, fifty pounds of flour and four bushels of wheat" were the "endowment" of an Indiana academy for one year.[39]

One way of saving on operating costs and of earning money was to have the students work during part of the day in some productive capacity. The optimism of this idea was as appealing as it was unrealistic: the school would support itself by becoming self-sufficient and by producing marketable goods. Inevitably, an association backing the scheme—the Society for Promoting Manual Labor in Literary Institutions—was formed, and schools were founded in its faith. The

[38] See Miller, *The Academy System of the State of New York.*
[39] Mock, *The Mid-western Academy Movement,* pp. 50–51.

scheme, of course, failed, since part-time, unskilled adolescents were no match for their full-time, skilled, adult competitors. The "manual labor" schools, academies, and colleges managed to raise some of their own foodstuffs, but they were never able to cope effectively with their students' protests that they weren't coming to school to sully their hands at hard manual labor.[40]

There were other money-making schemes. Some states specified that certain fines and collections by local or county authorities should go to the support of academies. Income from the lottery was widely used in the South, the right to use it being granted by the state legislatures. Some academies added a variety of special fees to augment tuition. Some "sold" scholarships: in exchange for a large sum of money, the academy would waive tuition for several generations of students. This scheme might have worked if the initial capital had been invested productively, but too often it was sunk into building and running costs, leaving the academy without sufficient income to carry out its continuing responsibility of educating students who paid no tuition.

There were also indirect sources of aid. Academies sometimes used public buildings, thus eliminating a costly item from their budgets. In some regions, the requirement to perform certain public duties, such as roadwork, was waived for academy teachers and students. Most important, however, was the economy of inexpensive operation. Many academies could exist only if they contented themselves with marginal quality: with poor buildings, poor equipment, and poor instructors. The teachers, representing the largest item on the budget, could contribute most toward lowering operat-

[40] For the experience of the colleges in this matter, see Rudolph, *The American College and University*, pp. 217–218.

ing costs: the smaller their salaries, the smaller the deficit. As in the colleges and common schools, the teachers, by performing their tasks for a pittance, became the main source of financial support. The benefactions of the state and the income from tuition pale in comparison with their donations.[41]

IV

Optimistic and laissez-faire in the extreme are the only ways one can describe the curricula of the academies. Anything and everything could be put into a course, most often a six-week course. States, towns, and trustees rarely questioned and, with few exceptions, fully supported the academies' wildly expansive programs, in New York going from acoustics to Greek, Chaldee to needlework, English to phrenology, waxwork, conchology, and optics.[42] Not only were the curricula broad, but the students were expected to digest the entire fare. In 1828, Montpelier Academy in Vermont required the following for a diploma:

Orthography, Reading, Writing, Composition, Geography, Grammar, Arithmetic, Rhetoric, History of Vermont, History U. States, Elements of Gen. History, Logic, Moral Philosophy, Astronomy, Chemistry, Drawing, Evidences of Christianity, Natural Philosophy, Geometry, Algebra, Surveying, Mensuration of Surfaces and Solids, Linear Drawing.[43]

In 1843, the preceptor of another academy in the same

[41] Frederick Rudolph has fully documented this for the college in "Who Paid the Bills?" *Harvard Educational Review*, XXXI (1961), 144–157. The same argument, in somewhat different form, appears in *The American College and University*, Chapter 9.

[42] Miller, *The Academy System of the State of New York*, pp. 118–119.

[43] Andrews, *The County Grammar Schools and Academies of Vermont*, p. 163.

state cast some doubt on the effectiveness of such curricula:

> The old academy of our boyhood days was the hope of the common schools, and the main feeder of the college; but it was necessarily unsystematic, as a result of the irregularity of attendance. Well-arranged courses of study and a graded system of instruction were impossible. Most of the students came from the farm and workshop, with no preparation except such as they could get in the district school of that day, and they were compelled to work their way unaided. Hence they were obliged to alternate terms of study in the spring and labor in the summer.[44]

The pretentious curricula were taught by one or two teachers to a constantly changing group of students, most of whom lacked a sound grasp of the rudimentary studies. What paragons of scholarship these teachers were expected to be! They were saved only by the fact that virtually all the courses were taught from a text; the teacher had merely to hear recitations. Further, most academy students never really reached the more specialized branches, for they were still hard at work on their elementary studies.[45] The high-sounding curricula, then, were as superficially taught as they were pretentious, and they were the first target of those post-Civil War leaders who tried to define what the curriculum of the high schools should be.[46] By 1900, the large number of short courses covering a wide variety of subjects was seen in few American secondary schools.

[44] Hiram Orcutt, *Reminiscences of School Life,* pp. 25–26, as quoted in Andrews, *The County Grammar Schools and Academies of Vermont,* p. 172.

[45] Miller asserts that in New York, a state which provided well for its academies, "until 1875 from one-half to three-fourths of all the pupils enrolled in academies were studying elementary subjects" (*The Academy System of the State of New York,* p. 64).

[46] See, for example, *Report of the Committee on Secondary School Studies* (Washington, D.C., 1893), pp. 39–40.

Many academies avoided excesses, combining sensibly the traditional Latin-school curriculum with more practical subjects similar to those suggested by Franklin. Most often, two or more "tracks," or parallel courses, were defined, one for college preparation, one for prospective teachers, one for "life," and so forth. The student's course of study varied according to the track he elected: the college-preparatory course remained particularly narrow, the student spending several years almost solely on language study; a pupil preparing for "life" often dabbled in dozens of subjects.

Master Tisdale's school in Lebanon, Connecticut, is an interesting early example of a mixture of Latin school, private-venture English school, and academy. Alumnus John Trumbull recalled the institution, which he attended in the 1750's and 1760's, as "the best school in New England," drawing students from as far away as the West Indies. Trumbull read Greek at the age of six and was fully prepared for Harvard at twelve, but he remembered that "my good master Tisdale had the wisdom to vary my studies, as to render them rather a pleasure than a task." Latin, geography, ancient history, arithmetic, trigonometry, surveying, geometry, navigation, and what Trumbull impatiently labeled "&c., &c." were covered until "it was stated by my good master that he could teach me little more." Tisdale's school represents well the early blending of the Latin-school curriculum with those studies long the domain of the English school.[47]

The Phillips academies and other prestigious New England foundations that followed the modest one-man schools like that of Tisdale broadened their cur-

[47] Theodore Sizer, ed., *The Autobiography of Colonel John Trumbull* (New Haven, Conn., 1953), pp. 4, 9–10.

ricula little from the base of Latin, Greek, and arithmetic. This was primarily because these academies were principally preparatory schools to colleges whose course of study remained largely unaltered from the medieval model. The colleges thus influenced the curricula of those institutions sending boys up and prevented their indiscriminate expansion. But the pull away from the Colonial models was irresistible. In a law passed in 1789, the Massachusetts legislature required the town grammar schools to offer Latin, Greek, and English. The 1827 "high-school law" added to this list United States history, "general" history, bookkeeping, algebra, geometry, surveying, rhetoric, and logic.[48] The same liberalizing tendencies were seen in New York and other states, all of which officially confirmed the expansion of the curriculum to include studies more contemporary, if not bizarre, that is, English and history, if not conchology.

It is important to note that with the exception of the teacher-training course, the academies did not offer vocational programs. Franklin's "useful" subjects were still largely intellectual subjects. More specifically vocational work did not find a large place in the ante bellum academies. Courses in carpentry, ironwork, applied agriculture, and related areas appeared only occasionally. Navigation found a spot in coastal institutions, such as those in New England, and surveying—taught from a book—was evident as well. These two subjects, however, really constituted a branch of mathematics. By and large, the academic fare was that which lent itself to being written down, memorized, and recited. The academies were not training for practical skills; their

[48] Inglis, *The Rise of the High School in Massachusetts,* p. 53.

avowed aim was to provide "training for life," and this meant book learning.

Several special types of academies deserve mention. In marked contrast to the Latin grammar schools, many academies admitted girls along with boys or were established solely for girls. Schools like Science Hill Academy in Kentucky founded in 1815, Troy Seminary founded in 1821 by Emma Willard, and the Hartford Female Seminary founded in 1828 by Catherine Beecher provided an organized course for girls. What is surprising is not that their curricula contained the "ornamental" subjects commonly associated with girls' education—music, French, dancing, and the rest—but that these academies tried hard to copy the curricula of the boys' schools. It was a difficult struggle, and the question of the necessity for the intellectual training of girls was constantly being raised. A rather unkind view appeared in an April 1828 edition of the *Springfield Republican:*

At a Female Seminary in Connecticut diplomas, premiums and titles have recently been conferred upon several young Ladies for excellence in literary attainments. We presume the title of MRS. would have been more acceptable and if the preceptor of that institution would engage to confer this title he would not be wanting for scholars.[49]

The wags lost out, however, and the formal education of girls beyond the three R's was firmly established, at least for those of well-to-do families, during the nineteenth century. That the girls were to master the same sorts of subjects as the boys can be seen clearly from the course of study of the Albany Female Academy. In those institutions which were coeducational the courses of study for both sexes were almost identical. The belief in the

[49] As quoted in Vera Butler, *Education as Revealed by New England Newspapers Prior to 1850* (Philadelphia, 1935), p. 190.

value of education and the willingness of interested Americans to found schools affected girls as well as boys; and the female and coeducational academies which resulted were a milestone in the emancipation of women in this country. That the battle was won is demonstrated by the fact that the public high schools which mushroomed in most parts of the country after the Civil War were almost without exception coeducational.

Another type of "academy" was the preparatory department attached to a college. Those who so optimistically founded the colleges in the ante-bellum period assumed that there were secondary schools to supply them with students. In this they were often disappointed. While the existing academies prepared a large number of students, many did not prepare them well enough or at a sufficiently advanced level. Further, the academies were unevenly spread, and some colleges found themselves without any local secondary schools at all. Their response was to open their own; indeed, some of them enrolled more students in their prep departments than in the colleges proper. In many cases, the students arriving in these departments had barely a grasp of the alphabet, and the self-styled universities found themselves teaching reading as well as moral philosophy.

There were other types of academies representing special interests. The Roman Catholic academies are a case in point. They were clearly schools infused with a set of particular religious beliefs; that they were in many respects like nonsectarian institutions and that they often enrolled large numbers of Protestants are the most remarkable things about them.[50] Military academies were also established, particularly in the South. Several southern states formed academies around the

[50] See Murphy, "Pioneer Roman Catholic Girls' Academies. . . ."

state armories, the students serving as guards for the states' munitions. William Tecumseh Sherman, ironically enough, was the principal of one such school, the State Seminary of Learning and Military Academy of Louisiana (now known as Louisiana State University), at the time of the firing on Fort Sumter. And there were other special-purpose institutions, running all the way to Colonel Dick Johnson's Choctaw Academy, which with federal and Baptist funds helped serve the Choctaws, Creeks, and Pottawatamies for eighteen years before the Civil War.[51]

West Point itself deserves special mention. Founded in the 1790's to answer the need of the unprepared new country for trained military engineers, it was formally organized in 1802 as the United States Military Academy. Frankly modeled on French counterparts, it almost immediately became a center of studies not so much in the military as in the more purely scientific arts. Even by the beginning of Sylvanus Thayer's notable administration as superintendent, the academy was offering instruction in the sciences and modern languages on a par with that of the best colleges. West Point was an academy in the sense that it was organized for a purpose far more utilitarian than that of Yale, for example; but with respect to its scientific studies, it was an institution of significantly higher rank than most academies.[52]

The normal school was yet another type of academy, though many of the schools of that name do not fit our definition, broad as it is. While normal schools were of secondary grade, their curriculum was largely a re-

[51] See Shelley D. Rouse, "Colonel Dick Johnson's Choctaw Academy," in J. E. Bradford, *Education in the Ohio Valley Prior to 1840* (Columbus, Ohio, 1916), pp. 88 ff.

[52] See Sidney Forman, *West Point: A History of the United States Military Academy* (New York, 1950).

view of the common branches and a smattering of pedagogy; the wide course of study generally seen in the academies was absent. Further, many of the normal schools were founded under state auspices; these flourished (or, rather, marginally survived) while many of the similarly sponsored academies failed. States trying to erect common-school systems could see the obvious necessity for training teachers for them and thus kept up a small flow of money to the normal schools. The academies of no apparent direct use to the state had a harder task obtaining public funds.

Many academies had normal departments, one of the first being that at Phillips Academy, Andover. There, in 1829, Samuel Read Hall opened his Teachers' Seminary, which provided a course parallel to the classical one at the academy. At one point, the seminary offered no less than twenty-six subjects—"an effort was made, apparently, to satisfy every longing of the human mind," Andover's historian notes—but its curriculum gradually became a more standard English-scientific course and was absorbed as such into the academy proper in 1842.[53] Hall left his mark in a more permanent way, however, by publishing his *Lectures on School-Keeping;* this little book, widely used in the training of teachers during the nineteenth century, has a timeless, if quaint, wisdom about it. But many academies other than Andover continued to prepare large numbers of teachers for the common schools. Well over half of New York's schools had academy-trained teachers at the time of the Civil War.[54] One would guess that the normal course had appeal, particularly for women, since teaching was one of the few voca-

[53] Claude M. Fuess, *An Old New England School: A History of Phillips Academy, Andover* (Boston, 1917), p. 209.
[54] Miller, *The Academy System of the State of New York,* p. 171.

tions they could undertake if marriage did not beckon.

Why was not the curriculum of the academies even more "useful" than it was? Why did the classics fail to die out, Latin remaining one of the three most studied subjects in the curriculum? Here we come again upon the puzzling paradox that the unintellectual and practical American fostered intellectual and impractical studies. One explanation is that the American, while objecting to the class pretensions associated with classical study, still admired the man who had apparently mastered it, if only superficially. Knowledge of Latin lent stature, even on the frontier. The American had enough contempt for academic studies to encapsulate them in absurd six-week courses, but enough awe of them to teach these very courses. This confusion is still with us: how many today scoff at the educated man and yet struggle that their children can gain the respect awarded by our society to educated men? If education has symbolic value, this is often worth something in the marketplace: it provides one with a salable quality which, although rarely a specific skill, makes possible a step up in the world. This insight was not lost on the American, anti-intellectual though he might have been. Bookish studies, if not scholarship, had their place in the symbolism of Americans. Thus did they remain the heart of the curriculum, even in frontier academies.

V

Who were the students of the nineteenth-century academies? There were all kinds. Both sexes were enrolled. No one social class was exclusively represented, but the fact that most academies were boarding establishments meant that only the reasonably well off could afford to send their children. Rarely, however, were the pre-Civil War academies associated with social distinction, although the New England institutions were something of an exception to this generalization.[55]

Typical was Iowa's West Liberty Academy. It was situated in a town of five hundred and was designed, it was asserted in its catalogue, "to fit young men for College, either for admission to the freshman class or an advanced standing; to give a scientific training to those who do not intend to take a collegiate course, and to fit young gentlemen and ladies for teachers." Its three instructors handled a vast curriculum for 156 students.[56] The teachers, however outnumbered, were expected to act *in loco parentis,* and the boarding establishments were justified on this ground. "The recognition of the period of adolescence, in a system of education, demands a grade of schools in which the interest of the pupil in his own welfare is a consideration paramount to the parental will or dignity."[57] In a thinly settled country, boarding schools were essential, and the best known among them drew their students from all over the nation. Most, however, served a county or group of counties; others were day schools, at least in part, serving a more restricted locality.

[55] See, for example, Kenneth V. Lottich, "Democracy and Education in the Early American Northwest," *Paedagogica Historica,* II (1962), 234–254. It is true that until precise demographic studies of school population during this period are made, the relative "classlessness" of many of the academies will remain open to question. That the academies were assaulted as bastions of prestige as little as they were is evidence in support of my generalization.

[56] Aurner, *History of Education in Iowa,* III, 69–70. Note how the present "advanced standing" notion seems to have had forebears west of the Mississippi.

[57] Hammond, "New England Academies and Classical Schools," p. 427. See p. 138.

The students were hemmed in by rules and regulations, although the effect of such legislation was probably slight. The laws covering behavior ran the gamut: no "association with the opposite sex," "spitting," "slovenliness," "throwing snowballs," "tight lacing," or "having gun powder on the premises."[58] The students lived a carefully planned day: early rising, prayers, then breakfast, recitation, luncheon, study, some free time, then dinner, more study, and bed. The days must have been dull for many; the youthful capers which brightened them are clearly suggested by the stern and specific prohibitions in the rules of the schools.

Most academies would accept all students who could pay the fees, a rudimentary grasp of reading being the only academic entrance requirement. As late as 1897, an Indiana normal school put this in its catalogue: "A great many persons have a wrong idea about a Normal School or College. They think that only those well qualified can enter. We accept students of all grades of advancement. . . ."[59] This policy, rarely stated with such appalling candor, was adopted by all but the most lavishly endowed institutions, academies as well as normal schools, for the understandable fiscal reason that they needed tuition to survive. Thus, many academies were really more in the business of teaching the common branches than the subjects normally associated with secondary schools. Anyone could enter—and did.

Who were the teachers? Judging from the range of subjects that the one- and two-man staffs offered, one might suspect that they were a liberally and thoroughly

[58] These particular restrictions were found, among dozens of others, in Indiana academies. See Mock, *The Mid-western Academy Movement,* pp. 78–79.

[59] Mock, *The Mid-western Academy Movement,* p. 68.

educated elite. That they were not is obvious. More often, they were people with a minimum of training, who moved rapidly from job to job unable to make a go of any. Sometimes they were college students earning a few dollars during vacation or young girls doing a stint of teaching before marriage. They needed as much in the way of rules as did the pupils.

There were probably an equal number of men and women teaching in the academies. Few stayed more than a year or two. Montpelier Academy in Vermont, for instance, had thirty-two preceptors from 1805 to 1853, twenty-three of whom were ministers.[60] Montpelier was a well-known school; if the record was bad there, it must have been worse elsewhere. There were exceptions, of course, the most spectacular being Benjamin Abbott of Phillips Exeter, who remained at the helm of that school for fifty years.

Although the average academy instructor was a poorly educated transient, several individuals stand out as the best of their clan. Abbott was one. Another was Andover's Eliphalet Pearson. A third was Moses Waddel of Willington, South Carolina, whose log-cabin school produced John C. Calhoun (who entered the junior year at Yale direct from Waddel), Judge A. B. Longstreet, and many others. John Chavis was notable, since he was a Negro; and his school in North Carolina prepared many distinguished white men, including a governor and a senator.

Recitation was the prevailing method of instruction: the pupil memorized a portion of a text and dutifully repeated it to the teacher. The length of the academic session varied widely, running from a few weeks to fifty;

[60] Andrews, *The County Grammar Schools and Academies of Vermont,* p. 163.

and many pupils did not attend faithfully. This must have caused difficulties, and one wonders how much the pupils really learned. Apart from recitation, the most important activities were debate and public speaking, the training in these areas leading to "exhibition days," on which parents and local townsfolk came to hear the students perform. Outside the formal curriculum, debating and literary societies flourished in some boarding schools; Exeter's Golden Branch Society, for example, founded in 1818, could boast a library of fourteen hundred volumes, secret meetings, and a select group of twenty members. Formally organized athletics were rare, but most of the larger institutions arranged musical events. Life in the academies clearly must have been less varied than in today's schools.

VI

The age of the academies had ended by the close of the Civil War. In the following decades the number of academies and the number of students within them both declined, while the public high schools began their spectacular increase, doubling in number almost every decade. At some point during the 1880's, the high schools took the lead in the number of pupils they enrolled, and by the turn of the century, they were clearly established as the dominant institution of secondary education in the United States.

The academy failed because it was fundamentally a rural institution, a school uniquely appropriate for a population thinly spread. In the rural regions, a secondary day school had been out of the question, since there were only a few persons in any given area who, wishing higher studies, could reach a school and return home daily. In addition, the scattered and most often only moderately well-to-do people could not afford to tax themselves generally to support such studies. Their solution was the privately sponsored, if publicly encouraged and to some extent aided, boarding school.

This institutional form was inappropriate for an urban center. Here, there was concentrated sufficient taxable wealth to support studies beyond the rudiments. Here, there were enough people to fill a day establishment, one similar to the common elementary school. In addition, the inhabitants of the city and the large town were better able to release their children for schoolwork than were the farmers who needed their assistance in the fields. Facing the changes burgeoning industry was forcing on the society, they saw more reason than did the farmers for giving their children more extensive education. From the beginning, the large towns and cities had few academies, as we have defined them: they had either public high schools—institutions publicly supported and controlled, with academy-like curricula—or numerous small, private-venture "English" or "writing" schools, whose course of study complemented the classical curriculum of the town's public Latin grammar school.

The American population grew rapidly during the nineteenth century, more rapidly in many states than did the academies to accommodate it.[61] This growth was concentrated in the cities particularly; the industrial boom of the Civil War years heralded the decline of agrarian America and the rise of the urban center. The towns, now transformed into cities, were for the first time able to support public high schools. Indeed, the growth of the public high school corresponds exactly with the growth of the urban centers.

[61] Inglis, *The Rise of the High School in Massachusetts*, pp. 57–58.

The high school is a city institution. It evolved most frequently as the outgrowth of a common school and was started in response to local pressure, so that students might stay on for higher studies. The addition of Latin to the curriculum usually marked the arrival of the "high-school" department. Most "high schools" in the nineteenth century remained in the same buildings as the elementary schools.[62]

Those areas that remained rural gave up their academies slowly, and there are parts of Maine, for example, which still maintain publicly aided but privately controlled academies in place of public high schools. Working against the rural sections of the country in the 1880's and 1890's, however, was a serious depression, which hurt the academies. Money was less available, and young men and women often left the farms and went to the cities, where economic opportunities were greater. Some city high schools admitted country children, who commuted on the newly laid railways, but this practice was both expensive and of limited use. By and large, secondary education in the country areas languished, and a committee of the National Educational Association which reviewed the situation in 1889 came to this somber conclusion:

For all secondary education, the mass of the rural population is generally dependent upon chance, or the favor of some city. . . . With few exceptions no opportunities or inducements

---

[62] The extent of this practice is convincing proof of the high school's origins. In Connecticut, for example, of 59 high schools in 1893, only 9 had buildings separate from the elementary school. The figures for Illinois in 1896 reveal the same pattern: of 258 high schools, only 38 were in their own buildings. See *Report of the [Connecticut] Board of Education, 1892–1894,* pp. 132–133; *Twenty-First Biennial Report of the Superintendent of Public Instruction [of Illinois], 1894–1896,* p. 14.

worthy of the name in the way of secondary or higher education are offered the rural population.[63]

The alteration of society—the advent of urbanism—dictated a change in the form of secondary education after the Civil War. There was much rationalization accompanying it, however, the most common cry being that the private academy was undemocratic, while the high school was in tune with American ideals. These arguments have a hollow sound, considering the substantial early support popularly elected legislatures in every state gave the academy movement and the acceptance of the academies by many political leaders as an integral part of a state educational system. Yet times changed. Even though the Massachusetts academies had had their early critics, a joint standing committee of that state could in 1859 report as a long-held government policy with respect to the academies:

They were to be regarded as in many respects, and to a considerable extent, public schools; as a part of an organized system of public and universal education; as opening the way, for all the people, to a higher order of instruction than the common schools can supply. . . .[64]

Yet in 1873 a Massachusetts school leader would say of the academies:

They tend to destroy the high school. Both should be sup-

[63] James H. Canfield, "The Opportunities of the Rural Population for Higher Education," National Educational Association, *Addresses and Proceedings, 1889,* p. 387. Daniel H. Calhoun has pointed out to me that Canfield's findings do not fully represent the situation in those areas of the South where public boarding high schools were "replacing" academies in regions as yet unaffected by urban growth.

[64] Report of the Joint Standing Committee on Education (Massachusetts), March 30, 1859; quoted in the *Fortieth Annual Report of the [Massachusetts] Board of Education, 1875–1876,* p. 209.

ported; the high school per force, and academy by love, if the
people will. High schools fit young men for college that otherwise would not have gone; and fit others for practical work,
who would not go to college or academy. With the high school
at their door, poor boys go, for parents can afford their boy's
time. They could not pay his board at a distant school. . . .[65]

The boarding academy was too expensive and was unnecessary for the town boy.

What happened, then, to the academies? Fewer were
established. Massachusetts chartered thirty-two between
1831 and 1835 and only five from 1856 to 1860.[66] The
pattern is clear. Other academies simply closed their
doors and are today forgotten, since few records of them
remain, particularly if they had never obtained a charter.
Still others altered their form. Some became colleges, following a pattern of long practice. Hampden-Sydney College, Washington and Lee University, Davidson College,
the University of Nashville, and several others started as
academies. Many were absorbed into the public school systems, becoming high schools. In 1847, the Hartford
Grammar School became the classical track of the Hartford High School. Chester Academy in Vermont was
merged with a public school district in 1869 and was
officially legislated out of existence in 1876. Iowa's
Waukon Seminary was bought out by the public school
district in 1867. In New York, the Union School Act of
1853 encouraged mergers of two or more local public
school districts, which could then offer studies in "academical departments." These received state aid in the
same fashion as the private academies. The act also
allowed an existing academy to be absorbed into a
merged school district to serve as one of these "academical

[65] Joseph White, in debate at the 1873 NEA convention; National
Educational Association, *Addresses and Proceedings, 1873,* p. 43.
[66] Inglis, *The Rise of the High School in Massachusetts,* p. 46.

departments," thus becoming a public secondary school.[67] Some academies survived by altering their character and student body, becoming socially or academically exclusive. Various well-known New England academies took this option, choosing to become private college-preparatory institutions and drawing their students from a wide, even national, geographic area.

Thus did the age of the academies close. It began, spiritually, with the proposals of Franklin and ended with the explosive growth of the urban high schools. As institutions go, the academies held the stage but a short time. Yet in that time they were "wisely suited to the character and condition of the people among whom they are [were] introduced," the optimistic Americans of the early nineteenth century.[68]

The academies illumine well several of the American's peculiar characteristics: his happy faith in formal education as a means to improve all men, his concurrent belief that such education must be "useful," his further and still more paradoxical unwillingness to provide regular tax support for the institutions which he desired. The academies symbolized the union of all these. They were widespread nationally, the optimistic creation of thousands of optimistic local leaders. Their curricula were a blend of what tradition had made the symbol of education and what the nineteenth-century American thought useful. And they were ventures, not of whole communities, but of small private groups of persons and

[67] Reed, "The Period of the Academy in Connecticut," p. 199; Andrews, *The County Grammar Schools and Academies of Vermont*, p. 170; Aurner, *History of Education in Iowa*, III, 94 ff; Gifford, *Historical Development of the New York High School System*, pp. 60–61.

[68] Edward Hitchcock, *The American Academic System Defended* (see pp. 94–105).

were aided by public moneys only on an irregular, ineffective basis. Thus do they represent in bold relief the optimistic, individualistic, practical, unintellectual American of a now lost rural past.

BIBLIOGRAPHICAL NOTE

The fact that academies were not public schools goes far in explaining their neglect by historians of American education. As Bernard Bailyn has pointed out (*Education in the Forming of American Society* [Chapel Hill, N.C., 1960], pp. 5–15), educational writers have looked at institutions too much from the vantage point of their own professional interests—the building of a public school system. Most of the studies of the academy movement were written in the first years of this century, and the neglect and distortion of the history of academies dates from that time. Few historians have yet bothered to look for the uniqueness and significance of the academy movement irrespective of its effect on the development of public education.

Another difficulty has been that the best-known academies were often the least representative. To many historians hurrying over the nineteenth century, "academies" meant Andover and Exeter, and the New England models were made to serve for the entire country. As the following documents suggest, much of the earliest and most literate debate on the merits and shortcomings of the institutions was carried on in New England, but it is obviously misleading to assume that the college-preparatory academies of the Northeast represented the entire movement.

It should be clear from the speculative nature of much

of this essay that a detailed study of the academies has yet to be written. While Frederick Rudolph's *The American College and University: A History* (New York, 1962) covers the tertiary level and Lawrence A. Cremin's *The American Common School: An Historic Conception* (New York, 1951) deals with the primary schools, there is no book covering the intervening institutions, save Robert Middlekauff's *Ancients and Axioms* (New Haven, Conn., 1963); this, however, limits itself to eighteenth-century New England. Since 1900, historians have relied on Elmer Ellsworth Brown's *The Making of Our Middle Schools* (New York, 1903), and Brown's theories have remained relatively unchallenged over the years. Clearly a new approach is needed.

As will be apparent from the footnotes, the sources for the present brief essay are largely state histories of education, many of which are quite dated. Several of those not previously cited should be mentioned here: E. W. G. Boogher, *Secondary Education in Georgia, 1732–1858* (Philadelphia, 1933); Charles L. Coon, *North Carolina Schools and Academies, 1790–1840: A Documentary History* (Raleigh, N.C., 1915); Frederick Eby, *Education in Texas: Source Materials* (Austin, Tex., 1918); Orwin Griffin, *The Evolution of the Connecticut State School System, Particularly High Schools* (New York, 1928); Emit D. Grizzell, *The Origin and Development of the High School in New England Before 1865* (New York, 1923); Silas Hertzler, *The Rise of the Public High School in Connecticut* (Baltimore, 1930); James Mulhern, *A History of Secondary Education in Pennsylvania* (Philadelphia, 1933); Dorothy Orr, *A History of Education in Georgia* (Chapel Hill, N.C., 1950); and Claude M. Fuess, "The Development of the New England Academy," *Creed of a Schoolmaster* (Boston, 1932). Most

of these works are compendia of data rather than inter-
pretative essays.

Henry Barnard's *American Journal of Education* and
the too often ephemeral academy catalogues remain the
best sources. Various other journals and the proceedings
of organizations like the American Institute of Instruction and the National Educational Association are also
useful.

1. An English Forebear

Various commentators on academies have, over the years, taken pains to trace the "academy idea" to Europe, even as far back as classical Greece. While the question of origins can rarely be fully answered, the early American academies in New England were probably modeled in part on one or more English forebears, the best known of which was that conceived by John Milton and described in his Tractate in 1644. The Tractate was written in the form of a letter to Samuel Hartlib. Milton's curriculum, which included such systematic science as his day knew, represented a marked departure from the narrowly linguistic course of the ancient English grammar schools.

John Milton: *Of Education**
(1644)

I am long since perswaded, that to say, or do ought
worth memory and imitation, no purpose or respect
should sooner move us, then simply the love of God, and
of mankind. Nevertheless to write now the reforming of
Education, though it be one of the greatest and noblest
designs that can be thought on, and for the want whereof
this Nation perishes, I had not yet at this time been in-
duc't, but by your earnest entreaties, and serious con-
jurements; as having my mind for the present half diverted in the pursuance of some other assertions, the
knowledge and the use of which, cannot but be a great
furtherance both to the enlargement of truth, and honest
living, with much more peace. Nor should the laws of
any private friendship have prevail'd with me to divide
thus, or transpose my former thoughts, but that I see
those aims, those actions which have won you with me
the esteem of a person sent hither by some good providence from a far country to be the occasion and the in-
citement of great good to this Island. And, as I hear, you
have obtain'd the same repute with men of most approved wisdom, and some of highest authority among us.
Not to mention the learned correspondence which you
hold in forreign parts, and the extraordinary pains and

* Oscar Browning, ed., *Milton's Tractate on Education* (Cambridge, England, 1883), pp. 1–23.

diligence which you have us'd in this matter both here, and beyond the Seas; either by the definite will of God so ruling, or the peculiar sway of nature, which also is Gods working. Neither can I think that so reputed, and so valu'd as you are, you would to the forfeit of your own discerning ability, impose upon me an unfit and over-ponderous argument, but that the satisfaction which you profess to have receiv'd from those incidental Discourses which we have wander'd into, hath prest and almost constrain'd you into a perswasion, that what you require from me in this point, I neither ought, nor can in con-science deferre beyond this time both of so much need at once, and so much opportunity to try what God hath determin'd. I will not resist therefore, whatever it is either of divine, or humane obligement that you lay upon me; but will forthwith set down in writing, as you request me, that voluntary *Idea,* which hath long in silence presented it self to me, of a better Education, in extent and comprehension far more large, and yet of time far shorter, and of attainment far more certain, then hath been yet in practice. Brief I shall endeavour to be; for that which I have to say, assuredly this Nation hath extream need should be done sooner then spoken. To tell you therefore what I have benefited herein among old renowned Authors, I shall spare; and to search what many modern *Januas* and *Didactics* more then ever I shall read, have projected, my inclination leads me not. But if you can accept of these few observations which have flowr'd off, and are, as it were, the burnishing of many studious and contemplative years altogether spent in the search of religious and civil knowledge, and such as pleas'd you so well in the relating, I here give you them to dispose of.

The end then of Learning is to repair the ruines of

our first Parents by regaining to know God aright, and
out of that knowledge to love him, to imitate him, to be
like him, as we may the neerest by possessing our souls of
true vertue, which being united to the heavenly grace of
faith makes up the highest perfection. But because our
understanding cannot in this body found it self but on
sensible things, nor arrive so clearly to the knowledge
of God and things invisible, as by orderly conning over
the visible and inferior creature, the same method
is necessarily to be follow'd in all discreet teaching. And
seeing every Nation affords not experience and tradition
enough for all kind of Learning, therefore we are chiefly
taught the Languages of those people who have at any
time been most industrious after Wisdom; so that Language is but the Instrument conveying to us things use-
full to be known. And though a Linguist should pride
himself to have all the Tongues that *Babel* cleft the
world into, yet, if he have not studied the solid things in
them as well as the Words & Lexicons, he were nothing
so much to be esteem'd a learned man, as any Yeoman or
Tradesman competently wise in his Mother Dialect only.
Hence appear the many mistakes which have made
Learning generally so unpleasing and so unsuccessful;
first we do amiss to spend seven or eight years meerly in
scraping together so much miserable Latine and Greek,
as might be learnt otherwise easily and delightfully in
one year. And that which casts our proficiency therein
so much behind, is our time lost partly in too oft idle
vacancies given both to Schools and Universities, partly
in a preposterous exaction, forcing the empty wits of
Children to compose Theams, Verses and Orations, which
are the acts of ripest judgment and the final work of a
head fill'd by long reading and observing, with elegant
maxims, and copious invention. These are not matters

to be wrung from poor striplings, like blood out of the Nose, or the plucking of untimely fruit: besides the ill habit which they get of wretched barbarizing against the Latin and Greek *idiom,* with their untutor'd *Anglicisms,* odious to be read, yet not to be avoided without a well continu'd and judicious conversing among pure Authors digested, which they scarce taste, whereas, if after some preparatory grounds of speech by their certain forms got into memory, they were led to the praxis thereof in some chosen short book lesson'd thoroughly to them, they might then forthwith proceed to learn the substance of good things, and Arts in due order, which would bring the whole language quickly into their power. This I take to be the most rational and most profitable way of learning Languages, and whereby we may best hope to give account to God of our youth spent herein: And for the usual method of teaching Arts, I deem it to be an old errour of Universities not yet well recover'd from the Scholastick grossness of barbarous ages, that in stead of beginning with Arts most easie, and those be such as are most obvious to the sence, they present their young unmatriculated Novices at first comming with the most intellective abstractions of Logick and Metaphysicks; So that they having but newly left those Grammatick flats and shallows where they stuck unreasonably to learn a few words with lamentable construction, and now on the sudden transported under another climate to be tost and turmoil'd with their unballasted wits in fadomless and unquiet deeps of controversie, do for the most part grow into hatred and contempt of Learning, mockt and deluded all this while with ragged Notions and Babblements, while they expected worthy and delightful knowledge; till poverty or youthful years call them importunately their several wayes, and hasten them with the sway of friends either to an ambitious and mercenary, or ignorantly zealous Divinity; Some allur'd to the trade of Law, grounding their purposes not on the prudent and heavenly contemplation of justice and equity which was never taught them, but on the promising and pleasing thoughts of litigious terms, fat contentions, and flowing fees; others betake them to State affairs, with souls so unprincipl'd in vertue, and true generous breeding, that flattery, and Court shifts and tyrannous Aphorisms appear to them the highest points of wisdom; instilling their barren hearts with a conscientious slavery, if, as I rather think, it be not fain'd. Others lastly of a more delicious and airie spirit, retire themselves knowing no better, to the enjoyments of ease and luxury, living out their daies in feast and jollity; which indeed is the wisest and the safest course of all these, unless they were with more integrity undertaken. And these are the fruits of mispending our prime youth at the Schools and Universities as we do, either in learning meer words or such things chiefly, as were better unlearnt.

I shall detain you no longer in the demonstration of what we should not do, but strait conduct ye to a hill side, where I will point ye out the right path of a ver-tuous and noble Education; laborious indeed at the first ascent, but else so smooth, so green, so full of goodly prospect, and melodious sounds on every side, that the Harp of *Orpheus* was not more charming. I doubt not but ye shall have more adoe to drive our dullest and laziest youth, our stocks and stubbs from the infinite desire of such a happy nurture, then we have now to hale and drag our choicest and hopefullest Wits to that asinine feast of sowthistles and brambles which is commonly set before them, as all the food and entertainment of their tenderest and most docible age.

I call therefore a compleat and generous Education that which fits a man to perform justly, skilfully and magnanimously all the offices both private and publick of Peace and War. And how all this may be done between twelve, and one and twenty, less time then is now bestow'd in pure trifling at Grammar and *Sophistry,* is to be thus order'd.

First to find out a spatious house and ground about it fit for an *Academy,* and big enough to lodge a hundred and fifty persons, whereof twenty or thereabout may be attendants, all under the government of one, who shall be thought of desert sufficient, and ability either to do all, or wisely to direct, and oversee it done. This place should be at once both School and University, not heeding a remove to any other house of Schollership, except it be some peculiar Colledge of Law, or Physick, where they mean to be practitioners; but as for those general studies which take up all our time from *Lilly* to the commencing, as they term it, Master of Art, it should be absolute. After this pattern, as many Edifices may be converted to this use, as shall be needful in every City throughout this Land, which would tend much to the encrease of Learning and Civility every where. This number, less or more thus collected, to the convenience of a foot Company, or interchangeably two Troops of Cavalry, should divide their daies work into three parts, as it lies orderly. Their Studies, their Exercise, and their Diet.

For their Studies, First they should begin with the chief and necessary rules of some good Grammar, either that now us'd, or any better: and while this is doing, their speech is to be fashion'd to a distinct and clear pronuntiation, as near as may be to the *Italian,* especially in the Vowels. For we *Englishmen* being far

Northerly, do not open our mouths in the cold air, wide enough to grace a Southern Tongue; but are observ'd by all other Nations to speak exceeding close and inward: So that to smatter Latine with an English mouth, is as ill a hearing as Law-French. Next to make them expert in the usefullest points of Grammar, and withall to season them, and win them early to the love of vertue and true labour, ere any flattering seducement, or vain principle seise them wandering, some easie and delightful Book of Education would be read to them; whereof the Greeks have store, as *Cebes, Plutarch,* and other Socratic discourses. But in Latin we have none of classic authority extant, except the two or three first Books of *Quintilian,* and some select pieces elsewhere. But here the main skill and groundwork will be, to temper them such Lectures and Explanations upon every opportunity, as may lead and draw them in willing obedience, enflam'd with the study of Learning, and the admiration of Vertue; stirr'd up with high hopes of living to be brave men, and worthy Patriots, dear to God, and famous to all ages. That they may despise and scorn all their childish, and ill-taught qualities, to delight in manly, and liberal Exercises: which he who hath the Art, and proper Eloquence to catch them with, what with mild and effectual perswasions, and what with the intimation of some fear, if need be, but chiefly by his own example, might in a short space gain them to an incredible diligence and courage: infusing into their young brests such an ingenuous and noble ardor, as would not fail to make many of them renowned and matchless men. At the same time, some other hour of the day, might be taught them the rules of Arithmetick, and soon after the Elements of Geometry even playing, as the old manner was. After evening repast, till bedtime their thoughts will be best taken up in the easie grounds of Religion, and the story of Scripture. The next step would be to the Authors of *Agriculture, Cato, Varro,* and *Columella,* for the matter is most easie, and if the language be difficult, so much the better, it is not a difficulty above their years. And here will be an occasion of inciting and inabling them hereafter to improve the tillage of their Country, to recover the bad Soil, and to remedy the waste that is made of good: for this was one of *Hercules* praises. Ere half these Authors be read (which will soon be with plying hard, and daily) they cannot chuse but be masters of any ordinary prose. So that it will be then seasonable for them to learn in any modern Author, the use of the Globes, and all the Maps; first with the old names, and then with the new: or they might be then capable to read any compendious method of natural Philosophy. And at the same time might be entering into the Greek tongue, after the same manner as was before prescrib'd in the Latin; whereby the difficulties of Grammar being soon overcome, all the Historical Physiology of *Aristotle* and *Theophrastus* are open before them, and as I may say, under contribution. The like access will be to *Vitruvius,* to *Seneca's* natural questions, to *Mela, Celsus, Pliny,* or *Solinus.* And having thus past the principles of *Arithmetick, Geometry, Astronomy,* and *Geography* with a general compact of Physicks, they may descend in *Mathematicks* to the instrumental science of *Trigonometry,* and from thence to Fortification, Architecture, Enginry, or Navigation. And in natural Philosophy they may proceed leisurely from the History of Meteors, Minerals, plants and living Creatures as far as Anatomy. Then also in course might be read to them out of some not tedious Writer the Institution of Physick; that they may

know the tempers, the humours, the seasons, and how
to manage a crudity: which he who can wisely and
timely do, is not only a great Physitian to himself, and
to his friends, but also may at some time or other, save
an Army by this frugal and expenseless means only; and
not let the healthy and stout bodies of young men rot
away under him for want of this discipline; which is a
great pity, and no less a shame to the Commander. To
set forward all these proceedings in Nature and Mathematicks, what hinders, but that they may procure, as
oft as shal be needful, the helpful experiences of Hunt-
ers, Fowlers, Fishermen, Shepherds, Gardeners, Apothe-
caries; and in the other sciences, Architects, Engineers,
Mariners, Anatomists; who doubtless would be ready
some for reward, and some to favour such a hopeful
Seminary. And this will give them such a real tincture
of natural knowledge, as they shall never forget, but
daily augment with delight. Then also those Poets
which are now counted most hard, will be both facil
and pleasant, *Orpheus, Hesiod, Theocritus, Aratus,
Nicander, Oppian, Dionysius,* and in Latin *Lucretius,
Manilius,* and the rural part of *Virgil.*

By this time, years and good general precepts will
have furnisht them more distinctly with that act of
reason which in *Ethicks* is call'd *Proairesis:* that they
may with some judgement contemplate upon moral
good and evil. Then will be requir'd a special reinforce-
ment of constant and sound endoctrinating to set them
right and firm, instructing them more amply in the
knowledge of Vertue and the hatred of Vice: while their
young and pliant affections are led through all the
moral works of *Plato, Xenophon, Cicero, Plutarch,
Laertius,* and those *Locrian* remnants; but still to be
reduc't in their nightward studies wherewith they close

the dayes work, under the determinate sentence of
David or *Solomon,* or the Evanges and Apostolic Scriptures. Being perfect in the knowledge of personal duty,
they may then begin the study of Economics. And either
now, or before this, they may have easily learnt at any
odd hour the *Italian Tongue.* And soon after, but with
wariness and good antidote, it would be wholesome
enough to let them taste some choice Comedies, Greek,
Latin, or *Italian:* Those Tragedies also that treat of
Household matters, as *Trachiniæ, Alcestis,* and the like.
The next remove must be to the study of *Politicks;* to
know the beginning, end, and reasons of Political Societies; that they may not in a dangerous fit of the Com-
mon-wealth be such poor, shaken, uncertain Reeds, of
such a tottering Conscience, as many of our great Coun-
sellers have lately shewn themselves, but stedfast pillars
of the State. After this they are to dive into the grounds
of Law, and legal Justice; deliver'd first, and with best
warrant by *Moses;* and as far as humane prudence can
be trusted, in those extoll'd remains of Grecian Law-
givers, *Licurgus, Solon, Zaleucus, Charondas,* and thence
to all the Roman *Edicts* and Tables with their *Justin-
ian;* and so down to the *Saxon* and common Laws of
England, and the Statutes. Sundayes also and every
evening may be now understandingly spent in the
highest matters of *Theology,* and Church History ancient and modern: and ere this time the Hebrew
Tongue at a set hour might have been gain'd, that the
Scriptures may be now read in their own original;
whereto it would be no impossibility to add the *Chaldey,*
and the *Syrian* Dialect. When all these employments are
well conquer'd, then will the choice Histories, *Heroic
Poems,* and *Attic* Tragedies of stateliest and most regal
argument, with all the famous Political Orations offer

themselves; which if they were not only read; but some
of them got by memory, and solemnly pronounc't with
right accent, and grace, as might be taught, would endue
them even with the spirit and vigor of *Demosthenes* or
Cicero, Euripides, or *Sophocles.* And now lastly will be
the time to read with them those organic arts which
inable men to discourse and write perspicuously, ele-
gantly, and according to the fitted stile of lofty, mean,
or lowly. Logic therefore so much as is useful, is to be
referr'd to this due place with all her well couch't Heads
and Topics, untill it be time to open her contracted
palm into a gracefull and ornate Rhetorick taught out
of the rule of *Plato, Aristotle, Phalereus, Cicero, Her-
mogenes, Longinus.* To which Poetry would be made
subsequent, or indeed rather precedent, as being less
suttle and fine, but more simple, sensuous and pas-
sionate. I mean not here the prosody of a verse, which
they could not but have hit on before among the
rudiments of Grammar; but that sublime Art which in
Aristotles Poetics, in *Horace,* and the *Italian* Commen-
taries of *Castelvetro, Tasso, Mazzoni,* and others, teaches
what the laws are of a true *Epic* Poem, what of a *Dra-
matic,* what of a *Lyric,* what Decorum is, which is the
grand master-piece to observe. This would make them
soon perceive what despicable creatures our common
Rimers and Play-writers be, and shew them, what religious, what glorious and magnificent use might be
made of Poetry both in divine and humane things. From
hence and not till now will be the right season of forming them to be able Writers and Composers in every
excellent matter, when they shall be thus fraught with
an universal insight into things. Or whether they be to
speak in Parliament or Counsel, honour and attention
would be waiting on their lips. There would then

also appear in Pulpits other Visages, other gestures, and stuff otherwise wrought then what we now sit under, oft times to as great a trial of our patience as any other that they preach to us. These are the Studies wherein our noble and our gentle Youth ought to bestow their time in a disciplinary way from twelve to one and twenty; unless they rely more upon their ancestors dead, then upon themselves living. In which methodical course it is so suppos'd they must proceed by the steddy pace of learning onward, as at convenient times for memories sake to retire back into the middle ward, and sometimes into the rear of what they have been taught, untill they have confirm'd, and solidly united the whole body of their perfeted knowledge, like the last embattelling of a Roman Legion. Now will be worth the seeing what Exercises and Recreations may best agree, and become these Studies.

THEIR EXERCISE

The course of Study hitherto briefly describ'd, is, what I can guess by reading, likest to those ancient and famous Schools of *Pythagoras, Plato, Isocrates, Aristotle* and such others, out of which were bred up such a number of renowned Philosophers, Orators, Historians, Poets and Princes all over *Greece, Italy,* and *Asia,* besides the flourishing Studies of *Cyrene* and *Alexandria*. But herein it shall exceed them, and supply a defect as great as that which *Plato* noted in the Commonwealth of *Sparta;* whereas that City train'd up their Youth most for War, and these in their Academies and *Lycæum,* all for the Gown, this institution of breeding which I here delineate, shall be equally good both for

Peace and War. Therefore about an hour and a half ere they eat at Noon should be allow'd them for exercise and due rest afterwards: But the time for this may be enlarg'd at pleasure, according as their rising in the morning shall be early. The Exercise which I commend first, is the exact use of their Weapon, to guard and to strike safely with edge, or point; this will keep them healthy, nimble, strong, and well in breath, is also the likeliest means to make them grow large and tall, and to inspire them with a gallant and fearless courage, which being temper'd with seasonable Lectures and Precepts to them of true Fortitude and Patience, will turn into a native and heroick valour, and make them hate the cowardise of doing wrong. They must be also practiz'd in all the Locks and Gripes of Wrastling, wherein English men were wont to excell, as need may often be in fight to tugg or grapple, and to close. And this perhaps will be enough, wherein to prove and heat their single strength. The interim of unsweating themselves regularly, and convenient rest before meat may both with profit and delight be taken up in recreating and composing their travail'd spirits with the solemn and divine harmonies of Musick heard or learnt; either while the skilful *Organist* plies his grave and fancied descant, in lofty fugues, or the whole Symphony with artful and unimaginable touches adorn and grace the well studied chords of some choice Composer, sometimes the Lute, or soft Organ stop waiting on elegant Voices either to Religious, martial, or civil Ditties; which if wise men and Prophets be not extreamly out, have a great power over dispositions and manners, to smooth and make them gentle from rustick harshness and distemper'd passions. The like also would not be unexpedient after Meat to assist and cherish

Nature in her first concoction, and send their minds
back to study in good tune and satisfaction. Where
having follow'd it close under vigilant eyes till about
two hours before supper, they are by a sudden alarum
or watch word, to be call'd out to their military motions, under skie or covert, according to the season, as
was the Roman wont: first on foot, then as their age
permits, on Horseback, to all the Art of Cavalry; That
having in sport, but with much exactness, and daily
muster, serv'd out the rudiments of their Souldiership
in all the skill of Embattelling, Marching, Encamping,
Fortifying, Besieging and Battering, with all the helps
of ancient and modern stratagems, *Tacticks* and warlike
maxims, they may as it were out of a long War come
forth renowned and perfect Commanders in the service
of their Country. They would not then, if they were
trusted with fair and hopeful armies, suffer them for
want of just and wise discipline to shed away from about
them like sick feathers, though they be never so oft
suppli'd: they would not suffer their empty and un-
recrutible Colonels of twenty men in a Company to
quaff out, or convey into secret hoards, the wages of a
delusive list, and a miserable remnant: yet in the mean
while to be over-master'd with a score or two of drunk-
ards, the only souldery left about them, or else to
comply with all rapines and violences. No certainly, if
they knew ought of that knowledge that belongs to good
men or good Governours, they would not suffer these
things. But to return to our own institute, besides these
constant exercises at home, there is another opportunity
of gaining experience to be won from pleasure it self
abroad; In those vernal seasons of the year, when the
air is calm and pleasant, it were an injury and sullen-
ness against nature not to go out, and see her riches, and

partake in her rejoycing with Heaven and Earth. I should not therefore be a perswader to them of studying much then, after two or three year that they have well laid their grounds, but to ride out in Companies with prudent and staid Guides, to all the quarters of the Land: learning and observing all places of strength, all commodities of building and of soil, for Towns and Tillage, Harbours and Ports for Trade. Sometimes taking Sea as far as to our Navy, to learn there also what they can in the practical knowledge of sailing and of Sea-fight. These ways would try all their peculiar gifts of Nature, and if there were any secret excellence among them, would fetch it out, and give it fair opportunities to advance it self by, which could not but mightily redound to the good of this Nation, and bring into fashion again those old admired Vertues and Excellencies, with far more advantage now in this purity of Christian knowledge. Nor shall we then need the *Monsieurs* of *Paris* to take our hopefull Youth into their slight and prodigal custodies and send them over back again transform'd into Mimicks, Apes and Kicshoes. But if they desire to see other Countries at three or four and twenty years of age, not to learn Principles but to enlarge Experience, and make wise observation, they will by that time be such as shall deserve the regard and honour of all men where they pass, and the society and friendship of those in all places who are best and most eminent. And perhaps then other Nations will be glad to visit us for their Breeding, or else to imitate us in their own Country.

Now lastly for their Diet there cannot be much to say, save only that it would be best in the same House; for much time else would be lost abroad, and many ill habits got; and that it should be plain, healthful, and moderate I suppose is out of controversie. Thus Mr. *Hartlib,* you have a general view in writing, as your desire was, of that which at several times I had discourst with you concerning the best and Noblest way of Education; not beginning as some have done from the Cradle, which yet might be worth many considerations, if brevity had not been my scope, many other circumstances also I could have mention'd, but this to such as have the worth in them to make trial, for light and direction may be enough. Only I believe that this is not a Bow for every man to shoot in that counts himself a Teacher; but will require sinews almost equal to those which *Homer* gave *Ulysses,* yet I am withall perswaded that it may prove much more easie in the assay, then it now seems at distance, and much more illustrious: howbeit not more difficult then I imagine, and that imagination presents me with nothing but very happy and very possible according to best wishes; if God have so decreed, and this age have spirit and capacity enough to apprehend.

2. Early Foundations

Two of the earliest efforts to found academies were those of Benjamin Franklin and the Phillips brothers. Their proposals called for institutions conducted under private auspices, whose curricula would be somewhat broader than that of the traditional Latin grammar schools.

Franklin's Proposals were published in 1749 in Philadelphia; the Phillips Academy Constitution was signed in 1778.

Benjamin Franklin:
Proposals Relating to the Education of Youth in Pensilvania*
(1749)

The good Education of Youth has been esteemed by
wise Men in all Ages, as the surest Foundation of the
Happiness both of private Families and of Common-
wealths. Almost all Governments have therefore made
it a principal Object of their Attention, to establish and
endow with proper Revenues, such Seminaries of Learning, as might supply the succeeding Age with Men
qualified to serve the Publick with Honour to themselves, and to their Country.

Many of the first Settlers of these Provinces, were
Men who had received a good Education in Europe, and
to their Wisdom and good Management we owe much
of our present Prosperity. But their Hands were full,
and they could not do all Things. The present Race are
not thought to be generally of equal Ability: For though
the American Youth are allow'd not to want Capacity;
yet the best Capacities require Cultivation, it being
truly with them, as with the best Ground, which unless
well tilled and sowed with profitable Seed, produces
only ranker Weeds.

* Leonard W. Labaree, *et al.*, eds., *The Papers of Benjamin
Franklin* (New Haven, Conn., 1959 *et seq.*), III, 397–421. Franklin's
lengthy footnotes are omitted here.

That we may obtain the Advantages arising from an Increase of Knowledge, and prevent as much as may be the mischievous Consequences that would attend a general Ignorance among us, the following *Hints* are offered towards forming a Plan for the Education of the Youth of Pennsylvania, viz.

It is propos'd,

THAT some Persons of Leisure and publick Spirit, apply for a CHARTER, by which they may be incorporated, with Power to erect an ACADEMY for the Education of Youth, to govern the same, provide Masters, make Rules, receive Donations, purchase Lands, &c. and to add to their Number, from Time to Time such other Persons as they shall judge suitable.

That the Members of the Corporation make it their Pleasure, and in some Degree their Business, to visit the Academy often, encourage and countenance the Youth, countenance and assist the Masters, and by all Means in their Power advance the Usefulness and Reputation of the Design; that they look on the Students as in some Sort their Children, treat them with Familiarity and Affection, and when they have behav'd well, and gone through their Studies, and are to enter the World, zealously unite, and make all the Interest that can be made to establish them, whether in Business, Offices, Marriages, or any other Thing for their Advantage, preferably to all other Persons whatsoever even of equal Merit.

And if Men may, and frequently do, catch such a Taste for cultivating Flowers, for Planting, Grafting, Inoculating, and the like, as to despise all other Amusements for their Sake, why may not we expect they should acquire a Relish for that *more useful* Culture of young Minds. Thompson says,

'Tis Joy to see the human Blossoms blow,
When infant Reason grows apace, and calls
For the kind Hand of an assiduous Care;
Delightful Task! to rear the tender Thought,
To teach the young Idea how to shoot,
To pour the fresh Instruction o'er the Mind,
To breathe th' enliv'ning Spirit, and to fix
The generous Purpose in the glowing Breast.

That a House be provided for the ACADEMY, if not in the Town, not many Miles from it; the Situation high and dry, and if it may be, not far from a River, having a Garden, Orchard, Meadow, and a Field or two.

That the House be furnished with a Library (if in the Country, if in the Town, the Town Libraries may serve) with Maps of all Countries, Globes, some mathematical Instruments, an Apparatus for Experiments in Natural Philosophy, and for Mechanics; Prints, of all Kinds, Prospects, Buildings, Machines, &c.

That the RECTOR be a Man of good Understanding, good Morals, diligent and patient, learn'd in the Languages and Sciences, and a correct pure Speaker and Writer of the English Tongue; to have such Tutors under him as shall be necessary.

That the boarding Scholars diet together, plainly, temperately, and frugally.

That to keep them in Health, and to strengthen and render active their Bodies, they be frequently exercis'd in Running, Leaping, Wrestling, and Swimming, &c.

That they have peculiar Habits to distinguish them from other Youth, if the Academy be in or near the Town; for this, among other Reasons, that their Behaviour may be the better observed.

As to their STUDIES, it would be well if they could be taught *every Thing* that is useful, and *every Thing* that is ornamental: But Art is long, and their Time is short. It is therefore propos'd that they learn those

Things that are likely to be *most useful* and *most ornamental,* Regard being had to the several Professions for
which they are intended.

All should be taught to write a *fair Hand,* and swift,
as that is useful to All. And with it may be learnt something of *Drawing,* by Imitation of Prints, and some of
the first Principles of Perspective.

Arithmetick, Accounts, and some of the first Principles
of *Geometry* and *Astronomy.*

The English Language might be taught by Grammar;
in which some of our best Writers, as Tillotson, Addison, Pope, Algernon Sidney, Cato's Letters, &c. should
be Classicks: The *Stiles* principally to be cultivated,
being the *clear* and the *concise.* Reading should also be
taught, and pronouncing, properly, distinctly, emphati-
cally; not with an even Tone, which *under-does,* nor a
theatrical, which *over-does* Nature.

To form their Stile, they should be put on Writing
Letters to each other, making Abstracts of what they
read; or writing the same Things in their own Words;
telling or writing Stories lately read, in their own Ex-
pressions. All to be revis'd and corrected by the Tutor,
who should give his Reasons, explain the Force and
Import of Words, &c.

To form their Pronunciation, they may be put on
making Declamations, repeating Speeches, delivering
Orations, &c. The Tutor assisting at the Rehearsals,
teaching, advising, correcting their Accent, &c.

But if HISTORY be made a constant Part of their
Reading, such as the Translations of the Greek and
Roman Historians, and the modern Histories of antient
Greece and Rome, &c. may not almost all Kinds of
useful Knowledge be that Way introduc'd to Advantage,
and with Pleasure to the Student? As

GEOGRAPHY, by reading with Maps, and being required to point out the Places *where* the greatest Actions were done, to give their old and new Names, with the Bounds, Situation, Extent of the Countries concern'd, &c.

CHRONOLOGY, by the Help of Helvicus or some other Writer of the Kind, who will enable them to tell *when* those Events happened; what Princes were Cotemporaries, what States or famous Men flourish'd about that Time, &c. The several principal Epochas to be first well fix'd in their Memories.

ANTIENT CUSTOMS, religious and civil, being frequently mentioned in History, will give Occasion for explaining them; in which the Prints of Medals, Basso Relievo's, and antient Monuments will greatly assist.

MORALITY, by descanting and making continual Observations on the Causes of the Rise or Fall of any Man's Character, Fortune, Power, &c. mention'd in History; the Advantages of Temperance, Order, Frugality, Industry, Perseverance, &c. &c. Indeed the general natural Tendency of Reading good History, must be, to fix in the Minds of Youth deep Impressions of the Beauty and Usefulness of Virtue of all Kinds, Publick Spirit, Fortitude, &c.

History will show the wonderful Effects of ORATORY, in governing, turning and leading great Bodies of Mankind, Armies, Cities, Nations. When the Minds of Youth are struck with Admiration at this, then is the Time to give them the Principles of that Art, which they will study with Taste and Application. Then they may be made acquainted with the best Models among the Antients, their Beauties being particularly pointed out to them. Modern Political Oratory being chiefly performed by the Pen and Press, its Advantages over the Antient in some Respects are to be shown; as that its Effects are more extensive, more lasting, &c.

History will also afford frequent Opportunities of showing the Necessity of a *Publick Religion,* from its Usefulness to the Publick; the Advantage of a Religious Character among private Persons; the Mischiefs of Superstition, &c. and the Excellency of the CHRISTIAN RELIGION above all others antient or modern.

History will also give Occasion to expatiate on the Advantage of Civil Orders and Constitutions, how Men and their Properties are protected by joining in Societies and establishing Government; their Industry encouraged and rewarded, Arts invented, and Life made more comfortable: The Advantages of *Liberty,* Mischiefs of *Licentiousness,* Benefits arising from good Laws and a due Execution of Justice, &c. Thus may the first Principles of sound *Politicks* be fix'd in the Minds of Youth.

On *Historical* Occasions, Questions of Right and Wrong, Justice and Injustice, will naturally arise, and may be put to Youth, which they may debate in Conversation and in Writing. When they ardently desire Victory, for the Sake of the Praise attending it, they will begin to feel the Want, and be sensible of the Use of *Logic,* or the Art of Reasoning to *discover* Truth, and of Arguing to *defend* it, and *convince* Adversaries. This would be the Time to acquaint them with the Principles of that Art. Grotius, Puffendorff, and some other Writers of the same Kind, may be used on these Occasions to decide their Disputes. Publick Disputes warm the Imagination, whet the Industry, and strengthen the natural Abilities.

When Youth are told, that the Great Men whose Lives and Actions they read in History, spoke two of the best Languages that ever were, the most expressive, copious, beautiful; and that the finest Writings, the most correct Compositions, the most perfect Productions of human Wit and Wisdom, are in those Languages, which have

endured Ages, and will endure while there are Men;
that no Translation can do them Justice, or give the
Pleasure found in Reading the Originals; that those
Languages contain all Science; that one of them is be-
come almost universal, being the Language of Learned
Men in all Countries; that to understand them is a
distinguishing Ornament, &c. they may be thereby made
desirous of learning those Languages, and their Industry
sharpen'd in the Acquisition of them. All intended for
Divinity should be taught the Latin and Greek; for
Physick, the Latin, Greek and French; for Law, the
Latin and French; Merchants, the French, German, and
Spanish: And though all should not be compell'd to
learn Latin, Greek, or the modern foreign Languages;
yet none that have an ardent Desire to learn them
should be refused; their English, Arithmetick, and other
Studies absolutely necessary, being at the same Time
not neglected.

If the new *Universal History* were also read, it would
give a *connected* Idea of human Affairs, so far as it goes,
which should be follow'd by the best modern Histories,
particularly of our Mother Country; then of these
Colonies; which should be accompanied with Observations on their Rise, Encrease, Use to Great-Britain, En-
couragements, Discouragements, &c. the Means to make
them flourish, secure their Liberties, &c.

With the History of Men, Times and Nations, should
be read at proper Hours or Days, some of the best
Histories of Nature, which would not only be delightful
to Youth, and furnish them with Matter for their Letters, &c. as well as other History; but afterwards of great
Use to them, whether they are Merchants, Handicrafts,
or Divines; enabling the first the better to understand
many Commodities, Drugs, &c. the second to improve

his Trade or Handicraft by new Mixtures, Materials, &c. and the last to adorn his Discourses by beautiful Comparisons, and strengthen them by new Proofs of Divine Providence. The Conversation of all will be improved by it, as Occasions frequently occur of making Natural Observations, which are instructive, agreeable, and entertaining in almost all Companies. *Natural History* will also afford Opportunities of introducing many Observations, relating to the Preservation of Health, which may be afterwards of great Use. Arbuthnot on Air and Aliment, Sanctorius on Perspiration, Lemery on Foods, and some others, may now be read, and a very little Explanation will make them sufficiently intelligible to Youth.

While they are reading Natural History, might not a little *Gardening, Planting, Grafting, Inoculating,* &c. be taught and practised; and now and then Excursions made to the neighbouring Plantations of the best Farmers, their Methods observ'd and reason'd upon for the Information of Youth. The Improvement of Agriculture being useful to all, and Skill in it no Disparagement to any.

The History of *Commerce,* of the Invention of Arts, Rise of Manufactures, Progress of Trade, Change of its Seats, with the Reasons, Causes, &c. may also be made entertaining to Youth, and will be useful to all. And this, with the Accounts in other History of the prodigious Force and Effect of Engines and Machines used in War, will naturally introduce a Desire to be instructed in *Mechanicks,* and to be inform'd of the Principles of that Art by which weak Men perform such Wonders, Labour is sav'd, Manufactures expedited, &c. &c. This will be the Time to show them Prints of antient and modern Machines, to explain them, to let

them be copied, and to give Lectures in Mechanical
Philosophy.

With the whole should be constantly inculcated and
cultivated, that *Benignity of Mind,* which shows itself
in *searching for* and *seizing* every Opportunity *to serve*
and *to oblige;* and is the Foundation of what is called
GOOD BREEDING; highly useful to the Possessor, and most
agreeable to all.

The Idea of what is *true Merit,* should also be often
presented to Youth, explain'd and impress'd on their
Minds, as consisting in an *Inclination* join'd with an
Ability to serve Mankind, one's Country, Friends and
Family; which *Ability* is (with the Blessing of God) to
be acquir'd or greatly encreas'd by *true Learning;* and
should indeed be the great *Aim* and *End* of all Learning.

Constitution of Phillips Academy*
(1778)

A short reflection upon the grand design of the great
PARENT OF THE UNIVERSE in the creation of
mankind, and the improvements, of which the mind is
capable, both in knowledge and virtue as well, as upon
the prevalence of ignorance and vice, disorder and
wickedness, and upon the direct tendency and certain
issue of such a course of things, must occasion, in a
thoughtful mind, an earnest solicitude to find the source
of these evils and their remedy; and a small acquaintance
with the qualities of young minds,—how susceptible
and tenacious they are of impressions, evidences that
YOUTH is the important period, on the improvement or
neglect of which depend the most important consequences to individuals themselves and the community.

A serious consideration of the premises, and an observation of the growing neglect of YOUTH, have excited
in us a painful anxiety for the event, and determined
us to make, in the following Conveyance, a humble
dedication to our HEAVENLY BENEFACTOR of the ability,
wherewith he hath blessed us, to lay the foundation of
a public free SCHOOL or ACADEMY for the purpose of
instructing Youth, not only in English and Latin Grammar, Writing, Arithmetic, and those Sciences, wherein

* *The Constitution of Phillips Academy in Andover* (Andover,
Mass., 1817).

77

they are commonly taught; but more especially to learn them the GREAT END AND REAL BUSINESS OF LIVING.

Earnestly wishing that this Institution may grow and flourish; that the advantages of it may be extensive and lasting; that its usefulness may be so manifest, as to lead the way to other establishments on the same principles; and that it may finally prove an eminent mean of advancing the Interest of the great REDEEMER, to His patronage and blessing we humbly commit it.

KNOW ALL MEN BY THESE PRESENTS, that we, SAMUEL PHILLIPS of Andover in the County of Essex and State of Massachusetts Bay, Esquire, and JOHN PHILLIPS of Exeter in the County of Rockingham and State of New Hampshire, Esquire, for the causes and considerations, and for the uses and purposes, hereinafter expressed, have granted, and do by these presents grant unto the Hon. William Phillips, Esq. Oliver Wendell and John Lowell Esquires of Boston in the County of Suffolk and State of Massachusetts Bay, the Rev. Josiah Stearns of Epping in the County of Rockingham aforesaid, Elias Smith of Middleton, William Symmes and Jonathan French, Clerks, Messrs. Samuel Phillips, jun. and Eliphalet Pearson, Gentlemen, and Mr. Nehemiah Abbot, Yeoman, all of Andover aforesaid, and to their heirs, all the Right, Title, and Interest, either of us have in certain parcels of land, hereafter mentioned, viz.

In three several pieces of land, situate in Andover aforesaid; the first of which contains about twelve acres, the second piece contains about twenty eight acres, the third piece contains about thirty acres, being lately part of the Estate of George Abbot Esq. deceased, and conveyed by Capt. Joshua Holt, Administrator on said Estate, to SAMUEL PHILLIPS Esq. aforesaid, March first one thousand seven hundred and seventy seven;—likewise two other parcels of land in said Andover, situate near the two first mentioned pieces, containing about thirty nine acres, conveyed by Solomon Wardwell to said PHILLIPS January twenty fourth one thousand seven hundred and seventy seven, together with all the buildings on said lands;—likewise two other pieces of wood land, situate in said Andover, containing about thirty two acres, conveyed by Nehemiah Abbot to said PHILLIPS January twelfth one thousand seven hundred and seventy eight;—likewise about two hundred acres of land in the town of Jaffrey in the County of Cheshire and State of New Hampshire, conveyed by John Little to said PHILLIPS September fourth one thousand seven hundred and seventy seven.

And the said SAMUEL PHILLIPS and JOHN PHILLIPS do also farther give, assign, and set over unto the said William Phillips, Oliver Wendell, John Lowell, Josiah Stearns, William Symmes, Elias Smith, Jonathan French, Samuel Phillips jun. Eliphalet Pearson, and Nehemiah Abbot, and to their heirs, the sum of one thousand six hundred and fourteen pounds, to have and to hold the same land and the same sum of money to them and to their heirs, to the USE and upon the TRUST, hereafter mentioned.

The lands shall be let out on proper terms, and the said sum of money put to interest on good security, or both improved in such way, as shall be found on the whole most beneficial; and the whole of the Rents, Profits, Issues, and Interest of said land, and of said sum of money, shall be forever appropriated, laid out, and expended, for the support of a public FREE SCHOOL or ACADEMY in the south parish in the town of Andover aforesaid in manner and form following.

The said SAMUEL PHILLIPS and JOHN PHILLIPS shall,

together with the beforenamed William Phillips, Oliver
Wendell, John Lowell, Josiah Stearns, William Symmes,
Elias Smith, Jonathan French, Samuel Phillips jun.
Eliphalet Pearson, and Nehemiah Abbot, be TRUSTEES
of said School; and hereafter the Master for the time
being shall ever be one of the TRUSTEES;—a major part
shall be laymen and respectable freeholders;—also a
major part shall not consist of the inhabitants of the
town, where the Seminary is situate.

The TRUSTEES shall meet on the last Tuesday of
April instant; and ever after, once in every year, on such
day, as they shall appoint; also upon emergencies, when
called thereto, as hereafter directed; and a major part
of the TRUSTEES shall, when regularly convened, be a
QUORUM; of which QUORUM a major part shall have
power to transact the business of their TRUST, except in
cases, hereafter excepted; and their first meeting shall
be at the dwelling house on the lands, purchased of
Capt. Joshua Holt, where Samuel Phillips jun. now
resides, at which shall be chosen the Officers of the
TRUST; a name shall be given to this Seminary and its
principal Instructor; and such other business, relating
to this Institution, transacted, as the TRUSTEES shall
think proper.

There shall be chosen annually a President, Clerk, and
Treasurer, as Officers of the TRUST, out of their own
number, who shall continue in their respective offices,
till their places are supplied by a new election; and,
upon the decease of either of them, another shall be
chosen in his room at the next meeting. The Master
shall not be chosen President, and no member shall
sustain the office of Clerk and Treasurer at the same
time.

The President shall, in all cases, give his voice and

vote in common with any other member; and, whenever there shall be an equal division of the members on any question, it shall determine on that side, whereon the President shall have given his vote; and in his absence, at any meeting of the TRUSTEES, another shall be appointed, who shall be vested with the same power, during such absence;—he shall call special meetings upon the application of any three of the TRUSTEES, or upon the concurrence of any two of the TRUSTEES in sentiment with him on the occasion of such meeting. And upon the decease of the President, a special meeting may be called by any three of the TRUSTEES. All notifications for special meetings shall express the business, to be transacted, if convenient; and be given at least one month previous to such meeting, if not incompatible with the welfare of the Seminary; and, when a special meeting shall be called for the appointment of an Instructor, or to transact other business of material consequence, information shall be given by leaving a written Notification at the house of each TRUSTEE, or in such other way, as that the President, or members notifying, shall have good reason to believe that each member has received the notice.

The Clerk shall record all votes of the TRUSTEES, inserting the names of those present at every meeting. He shall keep a fair record of every Donation, with the name of each Benefactor; the purpose, to which it is appropriated, if expressed; and of all Expenditures; and a true copy of the whole shall be taken, and kept in the Seminary, to be open for the perusal of all men; and, if he shall be absent at any meeting of the TRUSTEES, another shall be appointed, to serve in his room, during such absence.

The Treasurer shall, previous to his receiving the

Interest of the Seminary into his hands, give Bond for the faithful discharge of his office, in such sum, as the TRUSTEES shall direct, with sufficient Sureties, to the TRUSTEES of the Seminary for the time being by name; said Bond to express the USE both in the obligatory part and in the condition. He shall give duplicate Receipts for all monies received, countersigned by one of the TRUSTEES; one to the Donor, the other to be lodged with such member, as the TRUSTEES shall from time to time direct; and the TRUSTEES shall take such other measures, as they shall judge requisite, to make the Treasurer accountable, and effectually to secure the Interest of the Seminary.

The TRUSTEES shall let or rent out the lands in such manner, as they shall find on the whole most profitable. They may make sale of any kind of Estate, make purchases, or improve the property of the Seminary in any way, which they judge will best serve its Interest.

Upon the death, resignation, or removal of the Master, appointed by the said SAMUEL PHILLIPS and JOHN PHILLIPS, the TRUSTEES shall appoint another in his stead; and ever after from time to time, as there shall happen any vacancy in this office, they shall supply it.

Whereas the success of this Institution much depends, under Providence, on a discreet appointment of the principal Instructor, and the human mind is liable to imperceptible bias; it is therefore required, that, when any candidate for election, as a principal Instructor, is so near a kin to any member of the TRUST, as a nephew or cousin, in determining that election, any member, to whom the candidate is so related, shall not sit.

The TRUSTEES are empowered to appoint such Assistant or Assistants in and for the service of the Sem-

inary, as they shall judge will best promote its usefulness, and as may be duly encouraged.

No person shall be chosen, as a principal Instructor,
unless a professor of the CHRISTIAN RELIGION, of ex-
emplary manners, of good natural abilities and literary
acquirements, of a good acquaintance with human
nature, of a natural aptitude for instruction and government; and, in the appointment of any Instructor,
regard shall be had to qualifications only, without pref-
erence of kindred or friend, place of birth, education,
or residence.

The TRUSTEES shall make a contract with each Master
and Assistant, before their entrance upon office, as to
Salary; of which there shall be no alteration, but in
their favor; which the said TRUSTEES are empowered to
make, as to them shall appear reasonable, and as the
income of the Seminary will admit.

It shall be their duty, to inquire into the conduct of
the Master and Assistant, or Assistants; and, if they or
either of them be found justly chargeable with such
misconduct, neglect of duty, or incapacity, as the said
TRUSTEES shall judge renders them, or either of them,
unfit to continue in office; they shall remove the Master
or any Assistant, so chargeable.

The TRUSTEES shall determine the qualifications, requisite to entitle Youth to an admission into this
Seminary.

As the welfare of the Seminary will be greatly promoted by its members being conversant with persons
of good character only; no Scholar may enjoy the
privileges of this Institution, who shall board in any
family, which is not licensed by the TRUSTEES.

And, in order to preserve this Seminary from the
baneful influence of the incorrigibly vicious, the TRUS-

TEES shall determine, for what reasons a Scholar shall
be expelled, and the manner, in which the sentence
shall be administered.

The TRUSTEES at their annual meeting shall visit the
Seminary, and examine into the proficiency of the
Scholars; examine and adjust all accounts, relative to
the Seminary; and make any farther Rules and Orders,
which they find necessary, and not inconsistent with
any Rule, that is or may be established by the FOUNDERS.

They shall, as the Funds will permit, without affecting
the support of the Master or any Assistant, have power
to erect such buildings, as they may think necessary;
and at a convenient season, when of sufficient ability,
shall erect a large, decent building, sufficient to accommodate at least fifty Scholars with boarding, beside the
Master and his family; unless it shall be the determination of a major part of the TRUSTEES, that the true design of this Institution may be better promoted by the
Scholars boarding in private families, and by some other
improvement of the Interest of the Seminary. They
shall from time to time order such repairs, as they shall
judge necessary.

Upon the death, resignation, or incapacity for the
service, by reason of age or otherwise, of any of the
TRUSTEES, the remaining TRUSTEES shall supply the
vacancy by a new election.

In settling the Salary and Perquisites of the Master,
and in the consideration of every other question, in
which the Master is particularly interested, he shall not
sit. And, if any question shall come before the TRUSTEES,
wherein the Town or Parish, where the Seminary is
situate, may be a party or particularly interested, and
any Minister, belonging to such Town is a TRUSTEE; in
the consideration of such question he shall not sit.

At the meetings of the TRUSTEES there shall be made decent, not extravagant entertainment. Economy is to be ever viewed by the TRUSTEES and Instructors, in their respective capacities, as an object, worthy their particular recommendation.

The Master, when appointed, shall receive applications for the admission of Scholars, and determine them agreeably to the Rules, respecting the same.

He shall conform himself to the Regulations, established by the FOUNDERS and TRUSTEES, and have power from time to time to make such other consistent Rules and Orders, as he shall find necessary for the internal management and regulation of the Seminary; which Rules and Orders shall be subject to the examination, amendment, or discontinuance of the TRUSTEES, at their discretion.

It shall be ever considered, as the first and principal duty of the Master, to regulate the tempers, to enlarge the minds, and form the morals of the Youth, committed to his care.

There shall be taught in this Seminary the English, Latin, and Greek Languages, Writing, Arithmetic, Music, and the Art of Speaking; also practical Geometry, Logic, and any other of the liberal Arts and Sciences, or Languages, as opportunity and ability may hereafter admit, and as the TRUSTEES shall direct.

The Master is to give special attention to the health of the Scholars, and ever to urge the importance of a habit of Industry. For these purposes it is to be a part of his duty, to encourage the Scholars to perform some manual labor, such as gardening, or the like; so far, as is consistent with cleanliness and the inclination of their parents; and the fruit of their labor shall be applied, at the discretion of the TRUSTEES, for procuring

a Library, or in some other way increasing the usefulness
of this Seminary.

But, above all, it is expected, that the Master's attention to the disposition of the *Minds* and *Morals* of the
Youth, under his charge, will exceed every other care;
well considering that, though goodness without knowledge (as it respects others) is weak and feeble; yet
knowledge without goodness is dangerous; and that both
united form the noblest character, and lay the surest
foundation of usefulness to mankind.

It is therefore required, that he most attentively and
vigorously guard against the earliest irregularities; that
he frequently delineate, in their natural colors, the
deformity and odiousness of vice, and the beauty and
amiableness of virtue; that he spare no pains, to convince them of their numberless and indispensable obligations to abhor and avoid the former, and to love
and practise the latter; of the several great duties, they
owe to GOD, their country, their parents, their neigh-
bour, and themselves; that he critically and constantly
observe the variety of their natural tempers, and solici-
tously endeavour to bring them under such discipline,
as may tend most effectually to promote their own satisfaction and the happiness of others; that he early inure
them to contemplate the several connexions and various
scenes, incident to human life; furnishing such general
maxims of conduct, as may best enable them to pass
through all with ease, reputation, and comfort.

And, whereas many of the Students in this Seminary
may be devoted to the sacred work of the gospel ministry; that the true and fundamental principles of the
Christian Religion may be cultivated, established, and
perpetuated in the Christian Church, so far, as this
Institution may have influence; it shall be the duty of

the Master, as the age and capacities of the Scholars will admit, not only to instruct and establish them in the truth of Christianity; but also early and diligently to inculcate upon them the great and important scripture doctrines of the existence of One true GOD, the FATHER, SON, and HOLY GHOST; of the fall of man, the depravity of human nature; the necessity of an atonement, and of our being renewed in the spirit of our minds; the doctrines of repentance toward God and of faith toward our Lord Jesus Christ; of sanctification by the Holy Spirit, and of justification by the free grace of God, through the redemption, that is in Jesus Christ, (in opposition to the erroneous and dangerous doctrine of justification by our own merit, or a dependence on self righteousness,) together with the other important doctrines and duties of our HOLY CHRISTIAN RELIGION.

And, whereas the most wholesome precepts, without frequent repetition, may prove ineffectual; it is farther required of the Master, that he not only urge and reurge; but continue, from day to day, to impress these instructions.

And let him ever remember that the design of this Institution can never be answered, without his persevering, incessant attention to this duty.

Protestants only shall ever be concerned in the TRUST or Instruction of this Seminary.

The election of all Officers shall be by *ballot* only.

This Seminary shall be ever equally open to Youth, of requisite qualifications, from every quarter; provided, that none be admitted, till in common parlance they can read English well, excepting such particular numbers, as the TRUSTEES may hereafter license.

And, in order to prevent the smallest perversion of the true intent of this Foundation, it is again declared, that the *first* and *principal* object of this Institution is the promotion of true Piety and Virtue; the *second,* instruction in the English, Latin, and Greek Languages, together with Writing, Arithmetic, Music, and the Art of Speaking; the *third,* practical Geometry, Logic, and Geography; and the *fourth,* such other of the liberal Arts and Sciences or Languages, as opportunity and ability may hereafter admit, and as the Trustees shall direct. And these Regulations shall be read by the President, at the annual meetings of the Trustees.

Whereas, in the course of human events, the period may arrive, when the prosperity of this Institution may be promoted by removing it from the place, where it is founded; if it shall hereafter be judged, upon mature and impartial consideration of all circumstances, by two thirds of the Trustees, that for good and substantial reasons, which at this time do not exist, the true design, herein expressed, will be better served, by removing the Seminary to some other place; it shall be in their power, to remove it accordingly; provided that, if this event shall ever take place, there shall be fairly and truly entered on the Clerk's records all the reasons, whereon the determination was grounded; and the same shall be subscribed by the members, who effected the determination; but, unless the good of mankind shall manifestly require it, this Seminary shall never be removed from the South Parish in the town of Andover.

And we hereby reserve to ourselves, during any part of our natural lives, the full right, jointly to make any special Rules for the perpetual Government of this Institution; which shall be equally binding on those, whom they may concern, with any clause in these Regulations; provided, no such Rule shall be subversive of the TRUE DESIGN, herein expressed. We also reserve to ourselves a right, jointly to appoint one person, to succeed in the TRUST after our decease or resignation; to whom shall be transferred the same right of appointment, and to his Successors in the said TRUST forever.

In witness whereof we, the Subscribers, have hereunto set our hands and seals this twenty first day of April in the year of our LORD, one thousand seven hundred and seventy eight.

Signed, sealed, and de-   SAMUEL PHILLIPS (S.)
livered in presence of   JOHN PHILLIPS (S.)
  JOHN ABBOT,
  HANNAH HOLT.

3. Support for the Academies

At the dedication service of a new hall at the Williston Seminary in 1845, the Rev. Edward Hitchcock, president of Amherst College and a scientist, eloquently supported the academy idea. His speech was long— one can guess the discomforts felt by the boys of the academy, who were surely arrayed to hear the distinguished visitor—but it represents as clear a defense of the academy as was heard in the ante-bellum period.

Less sensitive but equally as strong a proponent was the Rev. Charles Hammond, principal of Monson Academy, who prepared a sketch of New England academies for Henry Barnard's first annual report as United States Commissioner of Education in 1868. One can infer from the categorical nature of his remarks the pressure that the public high school was already placing on the Massachusetts academies by the time of the Civil War.

Edward Hitchcock:
*The American Academic System Defended**
(1845)

Adaptation is the basis of nature's chief harmonies. If we examine an individual plant, or animal, we find its parts all fitted to one another with admirable skill. There is no clashing between them; no gap to be filled up; no superfluous member to encumber the rest. We shall find too, that the organic beings in a particular district of the globe, are adapted to one another, so that a proper balance is preserved among them. Then too, there is a striking congruity between the animal or plant, and the medium in which it lives, and the food it requires, as well as the climate that is natural to it. How beautifully adapted, for instance, is the eye to light, and the ear and the lungs to an elastic atmosphere! Nay, how obvious it is, that the motions of the heavenly bodies have reference to the wants and comfort of organic natures on the globe; since these motions bring about the seasons and day and night, just in the proper time to accommodate those natures. In short, creation is but a series of harmonies, produced by adaptation,

* *The American Academic System Defended: An Address Delivered at the Dedication of the New Hall of Williston Seminary, in Easthampton, January 28, 1845* (Amherst, Mass., 1845).

wheel within wheel in endless variety, yet all forming one vast and perfect machine. We do, indeed, sometimes meet with malformation or anomaly in a particular animal, or plant; and how struck we are by it, just because it is so uncommon.

If now we look at human society, we shall find that its elements, so far as nature has prepared and adjusted them, exhibit the same wise adaptation. But in the actual working of the system, we shall observe not a few instances of clashing, interference, and incongruity; because men pervert and abuse nature; or rather, because sin and ignorance have marred her fair features, and thrown down her landmarks, and put bitter for sweet and darkness for light. In some countries you will see governments entirely unadapted to the genius of the people; in others, gross superstitions keeping them in ignominious servitude to fear and fancy; in others, religions most hostile to light and knowledge; in others, systems of education which are better adapted to sink than to elevate the community; in others, absurd customs, which mar and debase the human character. In China and Papal countries, for instance, there is education enough to produce a gradual elevation of the community: but it has no adaptedness to such a purpose; and the public mind makes no advance. The Mahommedan religion inspires contempt for all infidels; and the syllogism by which Omar was led to burn the famous Alexandrian library, has, for more than 1200 years, shut up the Mahommedan mind in ignorance and self-conceit. "If these books," said he, "agree with the Koran, they are superfluous: if they disagree, they are pernicious and ought to be destroyed."

Probably in many cases the incongruous systems of religion, government and education, to which men submit, and the absurd customs which they adopt, are supposed by themselves to be well adapted to their condition. They cannot conceive why others should pity or ridicule them. They are in the condition of the queen of the Sandwich Islands, when those Islands began to emerge from barbarism, through the efforts of American missionaries. In that transition state, many most ludicrous mixtures of the savage and the civilized were exhibited. When the first horse and wagon were introduced, the queen, a personage of most portly dimensions, took a fancy to exhibit herself in the new vehicle to her subjects, and in a European costume. Adorning herself with a white satin dress, and placing a *chapeau bras* upon her head, she took her seat upon the floor of the wagon, and made a tour among her people. Surely, the sight must have severely tried the risibles even of the sober missionaries. Yet were the prayer of Robert Burns answered,

> Oh wad some power the giftie gie us,
> To see oursels as others see us,

I fear that some of the systems of education, and the customs and habits of civilized life, would appear as incongruous as this act of the island queen.

Ladies and gentlemen, I fear that my introduction will appear quite as poorly adapted to the occasion, as the dress of the Sandwich Island monarch. For my chief objects are, to bring prominently before you the principle, that systems of education ought to be wisely suited to the character and condition of the people among whom they are introduced; and then to proceed to show that the system of American Academies is well adapted to the character, habits, and wants of this country: and finally to point out some improvements which that system demands in its practical operation.

My first position, that systems of education ought to be wisely adapted to the character and condition of the people among whom they are introduced, need not detain us long. I have, in fact, already referred to one or two examples most pertinent to its illustration. I have said, that in China, no mean efforts are made in the cause of education; and though but comparatively few of her teeming population are devoted to a literary life, yet the most powerful stimuli are applied to raise the standard of scholarship, by conferring public honors on those who pass a satisfactory examination, and disgrace upon those who fail; and it may seem strange, that the minds thus stimulated, should not find that there is an outside to the nut shell within which Chinese intellect has been shut up for countless centuries. We should suppose that these minds would form a leaven, that must produce some heavings above the dead low level of custom and prejudice. But it is not so: and the reason is, that their plan of education is entirely unadapted to produce any advancement in human society; and therefore, as we view it, entirely unadapted to human nature; though in the view of the Chinese, this feature forms its chief glory. For two principles are so assiduously instilled into their minds from earliest infancy, that they seem to them *axioms,* which are fatal to any progress. The one is, that every thing out of the empire is barbarism, and to be despised; and the other, that custom is a sufficient reason for any course of conduct. To say nothing of other absurdities, these are sufficient to shut out forever the light of true science and religion from that vast empire, unless the missionary can dethrone them from their supremacy over the mind and the heart. Some who hear me, probably recollect the Chinaman that accompanied Dr. Parker to this country a few years ago. He seemed highly intelligent, inquisitive, and shrewd, on all common subjects. But when a friend of mine enquired of him in public, why the Chinese practised such an absurdity as compressing the female foot, he replied, with perfect *sang froid*,—"it is the custom:" and seemed as well satisfied with the answer as a mathematician would be with a demonstration of Euclid.

The other example to which I referred, was that of education in papal countries. It is well known that in some of these, the means of education are by no means deficient. In some sections of our country also, such as they are, they are abundant; and the papists consider their literary seminaries as a most important engine for spreading their peculiar system of religion. And indeed, in many respects their schools are models. In no schools are the pupils brought more directly under the influence and control of the teachers; and this is done too, in such a quiet manner, and so apparently by religious means, that usually the pupils feel unconstrained, and acquire a high regard and affection for their teachers. Indeed, if the advancement of the papal religion should be the grand object of education, this system is most admirably adapted for the purpose. But Protestants believe that the free developement of all the faculties in due proportion, and the means of examining all subjects impartially, in order to arrive at the truth, are the grand objects of education; and when the system does not furnish the means for attaining these objects, they regard it as fatally defective. Protestants intend that the pupils in their schools shall form their opinions, both in science and religion, from an intelligent examination of the subjects. Catholics too, are willing that their pupils shall learn Mathematics, Latin, Greek, and Rhetoric: but who ever heard of such a thing in them, unless forced upon them, as a free discussion of such points as the circulation of the scriptures, the infallibility of the church and the Pope, the authority of councils and tradition, and the right of requiring attendance at the Confessional? Such points are considered as settled, and woe be to the youth who should attempt to discuss them, or doubt them. If not driven from the seminary directly, he would soon find it so uncomfortable a place as to be glad to escape from it. In this country, indeed, papists are obliged to profess great friendship for public schools, and the circulation of the scriptures. Yet it is well known, that their secret feeling is the same as was openly expressed in early times, by a priest, when the Bible was beginning to be introduced into England. "Either we must root out the Bible," said he, "or the Bible will root us out."

With all his outlay, then, for education, the system of the papist is partial, and only those subjects are introduced, which will not throw any light, and have scarcely no bearing, upon the Catholic religion. And facts show that with a few exceptions, the system does not produce scholars of enlarged and liberal views; nor does it elevate the great mass of the community:—a point of prime importance in any system in a free country like ours;—in any system, indeed, in the nineteenth century. Admirably, therefore, as the system is adapted to sustain Holy alliances, the divine right of kings, and the supremacy and infallibility of Mother Church, it is utterly unadapted to this free Protestant country, as well as to this age.

I might proceed to show, that even when a system of education is good in its essential features, it requires modification to adapt it to different governments, and habits of thinking, in order that it should be most successful. And I might quote some systems, which, though they work well in Europe, cannot succeed in this country. But perhaps the discussion of the second position which

I have taken, will embrace all that is essential. I maintain
that our Academical plan of education, is peculiarly well
adapted to the genius, character, and government, of
this country.

The essential features of this system are, first, that it
affords an opportunity for youth of both sexes, from every
class in the community, to enjoy an elevated course of
instruction, on almost every elementary branch of science
or literature, to which they may choose to attend, and for
a longer or shorter period, as they shall wish: Secondly,
it enables those youth, who aim at the liberal professions,
or a literary life, to pursue a prescribed course of classical
studies, preparatory to an admission to higher seminaries.

Now I maintain, in the first place, that such a system
is well suited to the character of the government in this
country.

In most European countries, the education of the people is almost entirely under the control of the government, and is used as an engine of tremendous power for
the support of the government; even in a country where
the schools are so admirable as in Prussia. Excellent
facilities for instruction are, indeed, provided in many
of those schools. But the course of study is rigidly prescribed; and the youth who refuses to follow that course,
will be sure to fail of receiving the patronage of the
government; and to fail of this, is to fail of every lucrative
and honorable, I had almost said useful, situation. Now
this may be best for men living under arbitrary, or aristocratic forms of government. But in this country the
government presumes that every parent is intelligent
and judicious enough to judge what sort of an education
it is best to give his children; and, therefore, it leaves the
community to establish such seminaries as it pleases; ex-
tending to them only its protection and occasional pecu-

niary aid. It never enquires where or how a man was educated, in order to judge whether he is eligible to a post
of honor or profit; but only whether he *is* educated. The
people know this; and, therefore, if the government undertake to establish and control literary institutions,
which do not suit them, they neglect such seminaries and
set up others. Indeed, I know of no case in which an institution has been started and controlled by the government of a state, or of the United States, that has had any
thing more than an ephemeral success. It may be liberally
endowed, and supplied with able instructors, and a pro-
fusion of libraries and apparatus. But a free and intelligent people prefer to have the control of so important a
business themselves; and it has come to be pretty well
understood, that if we wish to have an institution fail,
let the government start it and attempt to support it.
And it would seem as if the government itself had learnt
this truth, and dreaded to make another attempt. I know
not how else to account for it, that the magnificent bequest of Mr. Smithson, has been of no service for seven
years, except to bring out occasionally an able report
from the venerable patriot of Quincy, or to furnish a fine
topic for speeches, and to make up for the deficiency
of slave labor and state funds in Arkansas. But had Mr.
Smithson understood the character of this country better,
and had committed his funds to the management of individuals, long ago would their fruits have been seen in the
establishment of a flourishing and useful institution.
The princely bequest of Girard seems destined to furnish
another illustration of my subject, because put under the
control of a city government; and because also, the donor
has attempted another impossibility, viz., to establish
a literary institution in this Christian country without
religion.

Now our Academical system of instruction chimes in admirably with this freedom from governmental interference with our literary institutions. Indeed, it originated in the fact, that the people were left in this matter to do as they pleased. They chose to establish schools, where they could have their children taught what they pleased, and as much as they pleased. This freedom has, indeed, produced some rather curious results: for we find that almost every village and several religious sects, have established academies, chiefly for the purpose of building up their own towns, or denominations. And yet, such institutions usually flourish better than any others, because they have more to sustain them, who are willing to make almost any sacrifice to render them attractive; and as to their sectarian efforts to attach the pupils to a particular party, they have little effect in a country where all matters are openly and freely discussed; and upon the whole, when we hear of a Baptist Academy, or a Methodist Academy, or an Episcopal Academy, or a Presbyterian Academy, we may pretty safely conclude that they are institutions well organized and efficient, because got up by enterprising and persevering individuals. Were the government to deprive individuals, or parties, or sects, of the right to establish such seminaries, their own forced treadmill system would be a wretched substitute.

In the second place, our academical system harmonizes well with the peculiar genius and character of Americans.

That Americans have a peculiar genius and character, is known all over the world. By Americans, however, I do not mean that motley crew, of all colors, and temperaments, and languages, and religions, which is annually disembogued upon our shores; but those in whose veins there flows some of the pure Saxon blood, that came over in the May Flower. If you meet with these men in any part of the world, whether as missionaries, or merchants in central Asia, or the islands of the Pacific,—as explorers amid the ice along the Antarctic continent, as whalemen on the coast of Greenland, or at the entrance of Behrings Straits, or as sailors in all seas and all climes, and you will meet them there, and almost every where else, you need not hear them speak to know that they are of Saxon origin, and have once trod the soil of the United States. Even John Bull, who amuses himself with yankee peculiarities, knows very well, that he must bestir himself, or he will be outstripped in enterprise, in industry, in arts, and even in arms, by brother Jonathan. If he does sometimes seem to be a simpleton;—if he has oddities, and even idiosyncrasies, they grow out of his condition, and command the high respect even of the very men who ridicule them.

One striking feature in the character of a true American, is a strongly marked individuality. I mean by this, that each man is in a great measure the architect of his own fortune and character. In many countries, especially those governed despotically, the great mass of men are very much alike, because moulded alike by external circumstances; and they seem to have little more of separate will, and a separate character, than the polypi that are united in building up a tree of coral. But not so with the American. Almost before he leaves his mother's arms, you will see a begun development of two things, that seem to be instincts. One is, a consciousness that he has got to depend upon his own efforts to establish himself in the world. Another is, a desire to economise every thing, so that there shall be no waste or superfluity. Very early he is apt to have his general course for life chosen, and then he makes every thing bear upon the accomplishment of his great object. He knows that a good education is essential to success. But he feels amply qualified, at least with the advice of parents and friends, to select the branches to which he wishes to attend, and to determine the degree of attention to be given to each. If he is looking forward to a literary or professional life, he consents to follow the course of study prescribed in the Academy, because he knows that he cannot otherwise enter the College: except that indeed, if he can so far make College rules bend, as to slide in with some deficiencies, he feels as if it were so much clear gain: although before he graduates, he usually changes his mind. But if he looks to any other business for life, he will not consent to have others tell him what course of study he shall adopt, and how far he shall pursue it. Hence our academic system exactly meets his wishes. Indeed, if it did not, he would not rest easy, till by union with others, he had established a system conformable to his views.

In the third place, our Academic system is well adapted to the wants of this country.

The literary wants of a country, comparatively new, where every thing is in a state of rapid progress, and where the elective affinities have not yet reduced to order the heterogeneous mass, are surely quite different from those of a people compactly settled, with habits and grades of society established, and surplus pecuniary means abundant. In the former, physical wants demand the first and usually the chief attention.—Yet men, of Anglo-Saxon origin at least, will not be satisfied even in such circumstances, till some means are provided, scanty though they may be, for the education of their offspring.—But it is chiefly the elements of learning that are demanded; and the seminaries of such a people must conform to those wants, only they should if possible be a little in advance of the state of society. Hence, in a country like ours, where every grade of society exists, from the well established organization of the Atlantic coast, to the log cabin of the back-woodsman, we stand in need of a corresponding grade of literary institutions for the great mass of the people. Our colleges and professional schools admit of being brought more nearly to an equality than schools of lower grade; and yet it is no disparagement to our western brethren to say, that the standard of scholarship, even in the higher seminaries is apt to sink as we go towards the setting sun. The same is true of our academies; and it seems to me one of the excellencies of the system, that they can conform to all the irregular demands of society, without destroying their individuality. If a fixed series of studies, and a fixed amount were necessary to constitute an academy, as it is essentially to form a respectable college, or medical, or theological, or legal institution, it would not meet the peculiar condition of our country, and of course, would not be patronized. In a country where all the pursuits and gradations of society are settled as if by a law of the Medes and Persians, which changeth not, and where men who venture beyond the primary school in their literary efforts, must depend chiefly on the government to reward them; and where indeed, it is extremely difficult for a man to rise higher than the government choose to have him, and where in fact the government chooses not to have the great mass of the community rise very high, it is practicable to have the course and amount of study graded as accurately as a railroad. But here the parent does not know what is to be the destiny of his son. For he is aware that the highest offices are open to talent and industry, even though blessed only with the education received in the primary school and the academy; and therefore he wishes that son to get some knowledge of the various branches of science pursued at the College and the University. It has, indeed, been said with much show of truth, that

> A little learning is a dangerous thing;
> Drink deep or taste not the Pierian spring.

But with us, the sentiment is, and it is a just one,—get as thorough an acquaintance as possible with that branch of knowledge which lies at the foundation of your business, or profession; but get also, a little knowledge, if you cannot get more, of as many other subjects as you can; and should you be called to the Presidential, or a gubernatorial chair, or to a foreign embassy, or to a place in the halls of legislation, or upon the bench, or into the ministry, you will find that all this little knowledge, instead of being a dangerous thing, will come into use most admirably. Now our academies, while they require a particular course and amount of study in some cases, can consistently, in general, allow their pupils a good deal of latitude in their choice, and also provide for those not aiming at a collegiate or professional course, that degree of theoretical and experimental instruction, which will give them a clear idea of the leading branches of science and literature. Now these glimpses into the arcana of knowledge, have often been the means of calling into action the latent powers of some of the most gifted and useful men of their generation. The European may, indeed, smile when told that one or two men are obliged to instruct in such a multitude of branches. But if this mode of instruction be actually needed by us, if it has trained up men able to cope with Europeans in all that is valuable, then let us not be laughed out of our system, and endeavor to substitute one which suits neither the genius, nor the wants, of our countrymen, however well it may answer for those whose lives are to be spent in rounding the head of a pin, or in tending a spinning jenny.

But though so well adapted to our free institutions, and to the genius and wants of our country, yet our academic system is liable to abuses; and some of these have actually been carried to a ridiculous extent. It is one of the excesses that grow out of the free and enterprising character of our citizens, that when one man finds out any employment that brings him either honor, or money, a crowd of eager spirits rush into the same pursuit, and so overdo it, that it soon ceases to be profitable or honorable. The same experiment has been tried upon our academies. In former days, these institutions were not numerous, and the government bestowed some largesses, by no means contemptible, so that they were able to provide respectable means of instruction; and they gave no mean reputation and pecuniary profit to the villages where they were located. As rival villages, however, rose up, they began to enquire why a similar institution might not be established among them. The result was, a great multiplication of these institutions, and a withdrawal of governmental patronage from them all, at least in most of the New England States. The citizens, however, found out that the academies, at least some of them, might nevertheless be prosperous: for neglect on the part of government in this country, usually stimulates individuals to greater efforts. Success, under such circumstances, only excited the enquiry among other villages, whether they ought not to have one of these institutions; and although many of them were too poor to provide any funds, yet they soon found out that this was unnecessary. They had only to obtain some young

man who was the owner, though not always justly so, of
a baccalaureate diploma, and some large room,—sometimes the dancing hall of a tavern, and then make an appeal to town pride, to furnish scholars. It was not necessary, nor wise, perhaps, to denominate such a school an
academy. But it was a select school, and had nearly all the
advantages of an academy. For could it be doubted, that
so eminent a teacher as had been engaged, was amply
qualified for unfolding the wonders of all science and
literature?

> The village all declared how much he knew:
> 'Twas certain he could write and cipher too.
> Lands he could measure, terms and tides presage;
> And e'en the story ran that he could guage.
> In arguing too, the parson owned his skill;
> For e'en though vanquished, he could argue still.
> While words of learned length and thundering sound,
> Amazed the gazing rustics rang'd around;
> And still they gaz'd, and still the wonder grew,
> That one small head could carry all he knew.

But to be serious, so great has been the rage for these
academies in miniature, that even though they can be
kept up only three months in a year, there is scarcely a
town in New England that is not provided with one:
nay, one is frequently provided for each parish in a town.
Now I will not deny that such schools do some good, and
enlighten some minds that would otherwise have remained in darkness. But their excessive multiplication
must lead men, in the first place, to neglect primary
schools; and in the second place, to undervalue and
neglect regular academies. What though these select
schools may be taught by as able men as the academies.
Yet it is a great mistake to suppose that able instruction
constitutes the whole of the advantages of an academy.

There is the stimulus which every virtuous son or daughter feels by being from home: there is the influence of new associates and new associations: the influence too of experiments in the physical sciences, and of libraries, and specimens, and many other influences, that make an academy a very different thing from a common select school, as those parents will find out at last, who make the latter a substitute for the former: or rather their children will find it out, when it is too late to apply a remedy.

I must notice another evil, which probably teachers realize more than others; resulting from that feeling of personal independence and supposed competence, which the American feels, to decide for himself as to the details of his studies. At the beginning of an Academic term, the teacher finds himself in the midst of perhaps a hundred pupils, of various ages, with most of whom he is unacquainted, and nearly all of them have got their course of study marked out, before consulting the teacher; although here they need instruction more than in any thing else. Frequently too, each scholar has chosen four or five studies, some of which he has attended to in part. Nor is he willing to alter his plans in the least, in order to be classed with others; especially does he regard it as insulting and so much dead loss, to go over any ground the second time. So that the teacher has the prospect of as many classes as he has scholars;—nay, three or four times as many; since each pupil means to attend to several branches; so that he seems compelled to give instruction on the principles of homeopathy. Well might he address his school, as Paul does the Corinthians: "How is it, then, brethren, when ye come together, every one of you hath a psalm, hath a doctrine, hath a tongue, hath an interpretation." If the teacher should add the apostles exhortation, "let all things be done to edifying," and proceed to bring order out of this chaos, he will find one and another crying out "well, if I cannot study what I wish, and as I wish,—if I cannot have any more attention, I will go to some other Academy, where I can do as I please."

Now this is really one of the most serious evils which the teacher meets in our common Academies: and it all grows out of an excessive development of the feelings of personal independence and self-reliance, for which Americans are distinguished. Nor can the evil be cured, until Academies are so well endowed and established, that the teacher can say to such unruly self-conceited spirits, "go away if you please; but we must and will have some system in our instruction."

I might proceed to point out other abuses and perversions to which the academic system has been subjected. But I prefer to ask your attention to some suggested improvements, which the system demands, in order that we may realize all its advantages, and correct its abuses; I mean improvements upon the more usual mode of sustaining and carrying forward these seminaries.

In the first place, these institutions should be more liberally patronized and endowed by the state governments, or by individuals.

This position is true in different degrees in respect to different parts of the country. For in some states, as in New York, Academies, and all other schools, do receive pecuniary patronage. But in New England, this can hardly be said, I believe of any state. Certainly in Massachusetts, whose policy in regard to literary institutions most concerns us, Academies as well as Colleges, have, for the last twenty or thirty years, been left to struggle on entirely alone. Primary schools, it is true, have received more favor; and this is well so far as it goes. Considerable sums have also been devoted to the enterprise of normal schools. I am not going to enter upon the question of the expediency or the value of such schools. But certainly they can be regarded only as an experiment; and while I would not object to the experiment being thoroughly made, it does seem a most suicidal policy, to lavish the resources of the state upon these schools, and to abandon to their fate, Academies and Colleges; whose value and importance have been established by the experience of centuries. It is easy to see, that where such institutions are not sustained by individual liberality they can have only a starved and doubtful existence; and cannot meet the demands for instruction of the nineteenth century. However successful normal schools and primary schools may be, this can not make up for a neglect of Academies and Colleges; because these institutions are demanded by the wants of the community, quite as much to say the least, as normal and primary schools. For the state to nourish the latter, and cast off the former, is just as if a man were to employ a surgeon to tie the arteries leading to his lungs and brain, and endeavor to force all the blood into the hands and feet. He might indeed in this way acquire extremities of huge dimensions, but they would become gouty and rickety, if there were only starved lungs to aerate the blood; and they would be clumsy and feeble, if the brain were so shrivelled that it could not impart the due nervous energy. So if the government persist in its throttling policy, in respect to Colleges and Academies, it will find the brain and the lungs of the state, ere long shrunk and feeble, and the extremities unwieldly and torpid. Or to drop the figure, it will find the higher branches of education suffering, and literary men lowering their standard of attainments:

and this will produce a reaction upon the elementary branches, and the general standard of literary attainment among us must sink. Indeed, under the blighting influence of such a policy, Massachusetts, now so proud of her fancied superiority to most other parts of the Union in the education of her citizens, must succumb to other states, especially to New York, where three dollars and a half are paid to her Academies annually, for every grammar scholar they contain, and her Colleges receive equally liberal benefactions. And we shall find ere long, that as the "star of political empire westward takes its way," so it will be with the star of literary empire. The only way to prevent such a result, is, for individuals of enlarged and liberal views, and adequate means, to extend that fostering care to our Colleges and Academies, which their unnatural step-mother, the Government, refuses to do. But how few possessed of the pecuniary ability, are themselves enough acquainted with literature, and have liberality of mind enough, to enable them to appreciate the wants of our literary institutions! If those connected with these institutions give a correct exposition of the means that should be possessed by such seminaries, their statements are regarded with extreme jealousy, as if these teachers merely desired to build up their own individual interests: and here too there comes in, with a most disastrous influence, that spirit of rigid economy which is so characteristic of Americans; and by such influence a majority in a republican government come to the conclusion that they must reduce to the lowest amount every appropriation to literary institutions: and in this State the lowest amount for the last thirty years has been just nothing at all. Really, when one contrasts such a niggardly spirit, with the noble benefactions of European governments and aristocratic individuals to literary institutions, it shakes his firmest republican principles, and he feels almost ready to come under an arbitrary government. At least, we cannot but regard it as one of the greatest evils of a popular government, that most of those chosen to administer it, have so low and inadequate views of what is wanted to make a College, or an Academy, what it should be. Nor can they be made to see, that by withholding their aid, and leaving these institutions to struggle on in poverty they are in fact cutting off the sinews of their own strength, and depleting their own veins. For whence do the sinews of a free people derive so much strength and nourishment, as from the intellect that is disciplined in their Colleges and Academies? It is easy to get up a prejudice against men thus thoroughly educated, as if they were aristocratic: but when the people come to look around for those who are to maintain their highest interests, whether in church or state, they are very apt to select those very men, and they take an elevated place in society just as naturally, as the tree that grows in the richest soil and is most cultivated, rises above others. The people never complain in such a case that a man is too learned, or his intellect too much disciplined; and yet when they come to consider whether the institutions that formed such men shall be endowed, they wisely conclude to starve them through fear of their aristocratic tendency.

In the second place, our Academies need buildings more substantial and convenient, and in better taste.

It will probably be thought by many, that the size, style, and finish of a building, intended for an Academy, can be a matter of no great importance, if it be only large enough for the purpose. At least when one looks at nine out of ten of the edifices devoted to this purpose, he must suppose such was the opinion of their builders. For if we meet in a village with a large edifice, destitute of all architectural beauty and proportion, and on nearer inspection, looking as if it had been devoted for years to the woodpeckers, or rather to the Goths and Vandals, he need hardly be told, that that is the academy. And on entering it, a stranger would infer that whittling and drawing with pencil, chalk or coal, must be among the branches taught, or at least practised, there. Foreigners, I believe, suppose that we need no teaching on these points, and that the disposition to whittle and deface objects, is so much of an instinct with Americans, that they are hardly to blame in the matter; and it is said, that in the public buildings of London and Paris, although no fears are entertained that Europeans will mutilate or deface any thing, yet to prevent Americans from doing it, small sticks are left here and there, on which they may use their penknives. And when recently I saw on Capitol Hill, at Washington, how the pedestal of the Herculean Statue of the father of his country was covered over with pencil marks, I felt a desire for some such device in this country as the Europeans are said to employ.

But really, if Americans do possess an unusual disposition for defacing and marring objects, it seems to me that it may in part be traced to the want of taste and neatness in our common school houses, and academies. Place a boy where every thing around him is rough and unsightly, and he will not easily restrain himself from depredations to increase the ugliness.— But place him in a room where every thing is in good taste, and well finished, and he will find it hard, especially if a hint be given him, to commence the defacement. And if he learns in early life to respect public rooms and public buildings, he will be apt in later years to keep his knife and pencil in their proper places. Can any one, who knows what unsightly and filthy places most of our common school houses, and many of our Academies have been, think it strange, that they have so often been marred and even riddled!

But there is another reason for the exhibition of taste and neatness in the construction of Academies. If so built, they will excite pleasant associations in the minds of pupils, that will never be effaced. Alas, many of us can testify that the opposite picture has left equally indelible associations, that are unpleasant. We recollect the Academies and school houses where we were educated, as huge piles of brick and mortar, or wood, devoid of proportion, or beauty, battered and torn on the outside, and cut and penciled and smeared over with dirt, on the inside; and however delightful the retrospect of those sunny days in most respects, the remembrance of those tenements, awakens little else but disgust and almost nausea. We cannot, indeed, at present in this country throw around our literary edifices so many interesting associations, as can be done in Europe; because there, the buildings are venerable often by their antiquity, and the remembrance of many a distinguished man educated there, whose departed spirit may be hovering around, gives a hallowed charm to the place. In 1843 for instance, the country school called *Pforta,* at Naumbourgh, in Prussia, celebrated its 300th anniversary, and eminent veterans of literature and science were there, to acknowledge their obligations to the place where they received the first rudiments of learning. I hold in my hand an able work on American Infusoria, presented on that occasion by Dr. Ehrenberg, one of the most distinguished philosophers of Europe.

But though we may not witness such celebrations till centuries have passed away, yet if our literary institutions generally were built more substantially, and in better taste, we might be sure to make those occasions more delightful for posterity, and accelerate the period when they may be held. Such buildings too, would inspire our youth with a correct architectural taste, as well as with habits of order and neatness, and their influence would soon be felt and seen throughout the land.

In the third place, our Academies need better elementary text books in science.

I understand that our elementary works upon ancient classical literature, are of a high order, and the same is true of some in English literature; but I hesitate not to say, that many of those in science, are far inferior to what they ought to be. I maintain that no man is qualified to write an elementary book upon any science, unless he has spent many years,—I had almost said most of his life,—in the study of that science; and has become somewhat eminent in it. If, with a superficial knowledge of it, he undertakes to give an exposition of its principles, he will be sure to present a distorted view of it. He cannot appreciate the relative importance of the principles of the science, and will consequently thrust some into bold relief, which should be kept in the back ground, and pass over others of prime importance. Now it is easy to show, that a large part of the elementary scientific works published in this country for Academies, are of just such a character. A single fact proves it. Their authors,—sometimes men and sometimes women,—have written similar treatises upon half the circle of science.—And to do this properly, demands nothing less than a prodigy of genius and learning. It would be prima facie evidence against a book, almost sufficient to justify an instructor in rejecting it, to learn that its author had attempted such a Herculean task. But were this the proper place, it would be easy to show also, that the works under consideration, although some of them have reached their fortieth edition, are full of misapprehension and misstatement of facts and principles, and of disproportionate views of the subject. And the only reason why no public exposition has been made of these errors, is, that the task of severe criticism is a most ungracious one. Probably the evil complained of, will continue, until men really qualified shall prepare text books, not as a money making project, which is now the grand stimulus, but from a sincere desire to place within the reach of our youth, the means of correctly understanding a favorite science.

In the fourth place, our Academies ought to be encouraged to raise the standard of classical attainment preparatory to admission to College.

The Colleges must, indeed, demand a higher standard of admission before the Academies can come fairly upon the ground proposed. But there are many arguments to induce the Colleges and Academies to unite in this enterprise: many arguments, I mean, that show the need of a more ample preparation than is now required for admission to College. With most of these arguments you are doubtless familiar. But there is one, which from my professional pursuits, has attracted my particular attention, and which I have not seen noticed. It is founded upon the fact, that with the present arrangement, only a single year in College is devoted to the entire circle of physical science. This vast field, so wonderfully expanded within a few years past, must all be gone over, or rather raced over, in this short period, because the other years are necessarily given to classical, mathematical, metaphysical, and moral subjects. Nay, these also are allowed to occupy nearly one half of the single year devoted to physical science. Now how preposterous the expectation, that in half or two thirds of a year, the student can master even the merest elements of some dozen or fifteen sciences, embraced in the three great divisions of Natural Philosophy, Chemistry, and Natural History! Indeed, he is hurried over them so fast, that often he does not learn that he knows nothing about them. And yet, at this day, when the community are ten times better acquainted with these sciences than they were twenty years ago, how contemptible will that publically educated man appear, who is ignorant even of their elementary principles. Under these circumstances, some would recommend that the study of the classics in College be abridged, and that of the sciences expanded. But waiving all other considerations, I should object as a naturalist to such an arrangement. For almost the entire classification and nomenclature of Natural History, are based upon Latin and Greek; and he who is ignorant of these languages, can make only a tyro in this study. And the modicum of this knowledge of the dead languages, usually acquired in a College course, is barely sufficient for the purposes of Natural History, and cannot be reduced consistently with a successful prosecution of that subject. More of the Latin and Greek, therefore, should be thrown into the preparatory course; and thus room provided for that more extended attention to physical science which is called for so loudly at the present day. When, therefore, we consider that this is only one of many arguments for a fuller classical course in the Academy, we cannot but hope that the day is hastening on when so desirable an object shall be accomplished.

In the fifth place, a more liberal provision should be made in our Academies, for the study of mathematics and the natural sciences.

By the natural sciences I mean Natural Philosophy, Chemistry, Natural History, and Geology. Now there is a great and increasing demand in the community for more facilities in the study of these branches. There are many, who do not wish to go through a collegiate course, because they are not looking forward to a professional life: but they wish and need elevated means of instruction. Some of them will become merchants, some manufacturers, some master mechanics, some agriculturalists, some captains or mates of vessels and steamboats, some overseers in factories, or engineers, and clerks on railroads, or in steamboats. Some will be elected to seats in the National or State legislatures: Some will become directors and overseers of Colleges and Academies, or of Railroads and Canals, and other great enterprises. Some will become Governors, Lieutenant Governors, Senators, or Councillors, or take high posts in the army or the navy. And what can such men do without a competent knowledge of mathematics and the physical sciences? Some, indeed, by indomitable industry and native strength of character, have reached those stations, though but slightly acquainted with these branches. But they feel more deeply than any others, their deficiencies; and lament that they are thus prevented from exerting that influence, or accomplishing that good, they might achieve, had their early education not been so defective. How very much cramped and mortified, for instance, must a man be, in any of the situations to which I have alluded, who has never studied Geometry, Trigonometry, Algebra, Spherics, or Mechanics. What can the man do, who is connected with railroads and

steamboats, or manufactures, if ignorant of chemistry and geology? or what scientific improvement can the farmer make, who understands not these branches? Indeed, to all the classes I have mentioned, the facts and principles of the natural sciences will be of daily use, and the man ignorant of them, cannot command the highest and most lasting respect of his fellow citizens, to say nothing of the great pleasure and moral profit derived from their cultivation. In short, if I may be allowed to quote the well known language of Cicero, all these classes of men may well say of these sciences:—
"Hæc studia adolescentiam alunt, senectutem oblectant, secundas res ornant, adversis perfugium ac solatium præbent; delectant domi, non impediunt foris; pernoctant nobiscum, peregrinantur, rusticantur."

Now I need not spend time in showing, that with perhaps a few exceptions, our Academies do not possess the means of giving this elevated course of scientific instruction. The recitation of limited and imperfect text books, with now and then an experiment clumsily performed, and the exhibition of a battered, poorly characterised specimen, will by no means answer the purpose. And not much more than this can be done in most of our Academies for want of means. They do not possess, and cannot obtain, the requisite apparatus, nor afford to their instructors the time necessary to classify specimens and prepare experiments that shall be elegant, satisfactory, and full. But why should not the men destined to occupy the important posts which I have mentioned, have the opportunity of witnessing experiments and illustrations of physical science, as complete and numerous, as the courses given in our Colleges and Universities? This would not convert, as some might imagine, an Academy into a College; but it would be only carrying out that fundamental principle of an Academy, which requires it to adapt its instructions to the wants of the community. Such a course would probably reduce the number of these institutions: because it would be only a few of them that are well enough endowed to give such an elevated and thorough course of instruction. But would such a reduction be an evil? certainly not if we include select schools under the term Academies: especially when we know that it would increase the respectability and usefulness of those that survived. Is not this elevation of their character the very thing that is needed by our Academies?

I have in the sixth place, only one other improvement to suggest, in relation to the management of our Academies. Yet this is more important than all the others; but I fear it has received less attention than any other, and that it will be more apt to be neglected in time to come; just because it relates to the spiritual interests of the pupils: and experience shows how prone we all are to place that last on this subject, which should be first. It does appear to me, that efforts as systematic and thorough should be made in our Academies, and indeed in all literary institutions, for promoting the spiritual welfare of the pupils, as for their progress in secular knowledge. I do not mean merely that they should be made intellectually acquainted with religious truth, for this is already done to a greater or less extent; but direct efforts should be made to make those truths result in their conversion and sanctification. In a word, the personal piety of the youth, should be made an object of efforts as systematic and thorough as their literary acquisitions. Now I believe I hazard little in saying, that such efforts rarely form a prominent part of the present mode of conducting our literary insti-

tutions. Every instructor feels it to be his duty to recommend personal piety: But this is usually done by occasional and irregular efforts; and hence it is too often
and sadly neglected. But suppose it were attended to as
systematically and thoroughly as the government and
literary instruction: would there not be reason to expect
that God would crown those efforts with as much
success as he does those for imparting literary and scientific knowledge. I believe that the connection of
means and ends is as certain and invariable in the one
case as the other. But in general, the impression has
been, that the chief object of a literary institution is
to impart secular knowledge, and that religion might
be put in a subordinate place. And is it to be won-
dered at, that God so rarely blesses religious instruction,
when it occupies only the second place,—a place, which,
by a decree of heaven, religion never can occupy? The
command is, *seek first the kingdom of God and his
righteousness* and all other things shall be added. If
this law of heaven is inverted, need we wonder that
so comparatively few students in our literary institutions receive those deep religious impressions which
result in salvation.

There is one circumstance that tends to make even
religious men, who found and conduct literary institutions, hesitate in their direct personal and systematic
efforts to lead the youth connected with those seminaries, to consecrate themselves to the service of God.
In a country like ours, most of these schools must
depend for their support upon the favor of the public,
and they are more or less rivals to one another. Now
there are some, in all communities, and even some respectable and professedly Christian men, who feel as if
very few direct efforts should be made to influence

the religious belief of young persons. All such efforts, they view as sectarian and bigoted, and maintain that youth should be left free, as they grow up, to adopt, without prejudice, those religious views which seem to them most reasonable; and that it is unfair for a religious instructor to endeavor to enforce upon his pupils his own creed, it may be in opposition to the wishes of parents. This would indeed be sound reasoning, were it not true, that youth have by nature so strong a bias against religion, that all the efforts of instructors, and even of parents, cannot produce a prejudice as powerful in favor of it; and after all is done, which devoted piety can do, the young heart will still remain so firmly braced against real religion, that there is need of a divine influence to overcome it. But some view all personal efforts to influence youth on this subject as an unwarrantable interference with the right of private judgment; and hence they will withdraw their patronage from the literary institution where this is done. To prevent this, the conductors of our seminaries are apt to lower their standard in this matter, and to persuade themselves that they may be excused from making religion as prominent as literature in their instruction. But in doing this, they forget that no Christian ought to expect God's blessing, if he does not let religion take the first place in all his enterprises. They forget, how easy it is for God to turn all their wise plans into foolishness. They forget, that *promotion cometh neither from the east nor from the west, nor from the south. But God is the judge: He putteth down one and setteth up another.* Hence the true policy of every literary institution is, to secure the favor of God, by honoring Him, and it may be sure of all the prosperity that will be best for it. And confident am I, that those seminaries will be most prosperous, that are most decided and consistent in their efforts to promote the spiritual welfare of their pupils. Let the trustees and instructors boldly declare their desire and intention to make vigorous efforts for the conversion and salvation of their pupils. True, here and there, in such a case, an irreligious man will refuse to patronise such an institution. But the great majority, even of men not themselves pious, are desirous that in this respect their children should not follow their example: nor will they be unwilling to have them come under a decided religious influence. We are yet, at least in profession, a Christian people; and, therefore, should we base all our enterprises upon religion. The few among us who are decidedly hostile to religion, can, if they please, attempt to found literary institutions where religion is excluded: But the signal failure of every such effort affords no doubtful intimation of the early result of all others of a similar character.

From all these considerations, then, we come to the conclusion, most decidedly, that in this Christian land, every literary institution is sacredly bound to give religious instruction a distinct, nay, the first place, in its arrangements: and that not only should it be acknowledged by instructors that the personal piety of their pupils is more important than every thing else, but it should be manifest in all their plans and arrangements that they really feel it to be so. Every Christian instructor will acknowledge that such a course would tend rather to elevate than to sink the standard of literary effort; because this is the order God has appointed: and experience shows, that when other things are equal, that man will be most successful in his intellectual efforts, whose religious affections are in the best state. On this point, then, it appears to me, that there is a great defect in most of our literary institutions. For in most of them the personal religious instruction of the pupils is left chiefly unprovided for; and in fact, only the shreds and patches of time are devoted to it; and it is attended to rather spasmodically than systematically. Oh that a reformation might be effected on this most important point! Then should we find our children issuing from the literary seminary, not only better scholars, but, in a majority of cases, decided Christians.

Ladies and Gentlemen, I present these suggested improvements in our system of Academical instruction, under most favorable circumstances. For in the institution at whose invitation we have assembled, we find them all, or nearly all, adopted, and already tested by successful experiment. We do not, indeed, see here the fruit of governmental patronage. Had its founders waited for this, I fear that the materials which now constitute these noble edifices, would have still remained unwrought in the mountains. But under a private patronage, truly princely, and far greater in amount than has been given by the government of Massachusetts to all her Academies and three Colleges for the last thirty years, have edifices risen in this beautiful valley, as if by magic, that will form a model for similar institutions through the land, and be remembered with pleasure by the numerous youth who will here lay the foundation of an education, that will qualify them for extensive usefulness. And those edifices have been provided with Chemical and Philosophical Apparatus so ample, and with specimens in Natural History so numerous and well characterized, as to leave little more in these departments to be desired. Here too, we find the standard of preparation for College as thorough as possible, until the Colleges themselves shall take higher ground. Nor do we find any connivance here, with those contraband efforts, by which very many young men are annually foisted into our Colleges, half fitted, only to become annoyances to their teachers, and to be themselves continually mortified, because they cannot take that standing to which their natural abilities entitle them. I am not indeed, familiar with the details of religious instruction in this Seminary, since these are labors which true piety does not proclaim upon the house top. But if it take that prominence, which I know the founder and teachers desire, in this respect too, will this Institution assume that preeminence which is accorded to its literary character.

In view of these facts, then, with great pleasure and strong hope, may we dedicate to-day, to the service of learning and religion, the new and noble Edifice which has just been added to this Institution. Nor is it without reason, or precedent, that this edifice is consecrated to these high purposes by public solemnities. For if men gather together to celebrate the launching of a ship, the opening of a railroad, the first trip of a steam boat, or even the completion of a private mansion, how much more proper, publicly to notice the opening of a costly edifice, devoted to purposes far more noble and important to the interests of the world, than the objects just named:—I mean the cause of learning and religion. Such dedications may not, indeed, be very common in this country; and our republican simplicity may lead us to undervalue them. But not so in Europe. I hold in my hand a Latin Oration, pronounced on such an occasion by Dr. Schweigger at Halle in Germany, agreeably, as he says, to a custom handed down from ancestors. A distinguished Academy had long existed in that city; and now that an important addition had been made to its buildings, it was judged that a Latin Oration should be pronounced; and no less than four degrees of Doctor in Philosophy, and Master of Arts were conferred upon the teachers, and other men of distinction. A leading object of the oration is to show, that the grand aim of establishing, not only the Academy at Halle, but most of the learned Academies and Societies of Europe, was to extend a knowledge of the Christian religion in connection with science to heathen nations. In view of this interesting fact, well does Dr. Schweigger remark, that the "dedication of the edifices of the Halle Academy, does not imply that the arts and sciences are to be shut up within the narrow limits of a school, or a kingdom; but rather, that from them much fruit should be imparted to the whole human family." This is, indeed, or should be, the grand object of every literary institution; and I trust I may apply it with peculiar emphasis to the Seminary in this place. Let not the inhabitants of this favored valley imagine, because it is located among them, and they can most fully enjoy its advantages, that it was intended exclusively for them. Nor let the population of this State, or of the United States, fancy that it belongs alone to them. I know that its founder and its trustees and teachers have consecrated it to the service of the human family. They mean it shall perform its full part in the grand work of enlightening and saving the world. Henceforth then, let no man, or body of men regard these edifices as belonging to them; but rather as sacredly devoted to the service of mankind. Justly, indeed, might we do honor to the munificence which has been so liberally lavished upon this great object. And yet, had I the power, I should feel that to confer a degree of Doctor in Philosophy, would be a most meagre reward, either to the founder or the teachers. I would rather repeat the words, written in Westminster Abbey, over the grave of Sir Christopher Wren, the architect of that splendid edifice:—"Si monumentum quaeris, circumspice." Nay, I would take a view still more congenial to the Christian heart. I would ascend the mount of prophecy, and catching the light which emanates from these foundations, I would watch its progress, as it struggles with the darkness of sin and ignorance; and I should see it widening and brightening down the track of the world's history, until, mingling with a thousand other lights, which learning and benevolence shall have kindled, the noon-day glories of a millenium of science and religion would encircle the whole earth.

Charles Hammond:
*New England Academies and Classical Schools** (1868)

No better proof is needed to show the value of the first established Academies, in their relation to popular uses, than the desire to multiply schools under that name in nearly all the important towns. This desire was prompted chiefly by the higher English education they furnished; making them, in all the towns where they were located, an important auxiliary to the elemental schools. Prompted by local enterprise, and aiming to secure the advantages which vicinity was supposed to give, schools called Academies sprang up in great numbers, having no endowments, without any other than a mere local policy, and with an irregular and intermittent existence; the patronage depending solely on the local popularity of the teacher.

In process of time, some of the older incorporated Academies, as Marblehead, Bristol, and Framingham, became local schools, and lost their former character as schools for the public at large.

As the wealth and population of the country increased, a demand was made for a higher grade of strictly local schools in all the larger towns, and for that

* Boston, 1877, pp. 25–35.

reason the unendowed Academies generally and very properly assumed the position and functions belonging now to the modern High School, which ought always to be supplementary to the Common School system.

Most unfortunately for the progress of popular education, some who have labored to extend the High School system in view of its transcendent utility, have assumed a position of antagonism to Academies, calling in question their policy, regarding their day of service as past, and advocating the substitution of High Schools in their place.

We most cordially sympathize with the expansion of the system of public instruction to the utmost limit of practical improvement. We fully recognize the advancement of popular education to that degree, that in many respects the local High Schools may be equal in rank to the condition and standing of the Academies in former days. But High Schools must, if they fulfil their proper design, be adapted to the wants of their localities, and meet the average standard which the people of each locality may have the ability and the will to reach. We care not how many such schools exist, or how high a rank of real excellence they may attain, for their object is to supplement the elemental schools, and their rank as *High* Schools is correlate to the lower grades in the public system of instruction to which they in common belong.

Of course it follows that the term High School is a very indefinite term, when regarded in its proper relation to the public system; since the High Schools of Boston and Salem and Cambridge must be at the head of a greater number of grades than in the country, where only two, or at most three, grades can be introduced. And yet the average capacity of pupils in the cities must be met as well as those in the country, and the range of studies must not be so high as to render the school of no use to those for whose sake it is specially designed. It is the grade of schools everywhere, and not the name, that confers on them real rank.

Now, it is clearly beyond the proper province, as it is beyond the ability of nearly all the High Schools, conducted as they are or ought to be in these days, to fit boys for "ye universitie" as the ancient Grammar Schools might do; since the standard of college education and of the preparatory schools is as much higher now than formerly, as is the rank of the best High Schools of our times above the elemental schools half a century ago.

Far better it is for the pupils who wish to prepare for College, and far more economical is it for the community, that the Academies should continue to do that work well, than that the High Schools should assume to do so great a work for so few in number, while the welfare of the great majority of their pupils is neglected.

In Boston and New York and large cities and towns, where wealth is abundant and the gradation of the Public Schools is perfect, the highest in the series may be a school preparatory for the University; for such places can well afford the expense, although the proportion of city boys who prepare for College is not one-half as great as it is in the country, and in the country not more than one in a thousand of the boys belonging to the Public Schools ever go to College.

The Boston Latin School, the oldest Grammar School in the land, has always sustained the very first rank as a classical seminary. It has for a constituency, one of the largest and most enlightened of American cities. The wealth of that city is equal to nearly one-

third of the entire valuation of the State of Massachusetts. The Latin School is the only classical seminary
in that city sustained by public taxation. It has the
best teachers which the highest salaries can procure,
and all the advantages which the best instruction and
the best discipline can give.

According to the Report of the Committee on the
Latin School of Boston (Dr. N. B. Shurtleff, chairman) to
the Boston School Committee, September, 1861, it appears
that the average number prepared for College, for the
ten years previous, at the Boston Latin School, was
16.8 per annum; and of these the average number of
those received from the Public Schools was 7.7, while
the number received from other schools was 9.1, making
the whole number 16.8 as the annual average of this
celebrated school, or seventy-seven who entered the
school from the Public Schools of the city, and ninety-
one from Private Schools. As to those who entered from
Private Schools, amounting to more than half of the
whole, it may be presumed that this great accession
from schools not belonging to the public system must be
due to the excellence of the Latin School, and the fact
that its tuition is free to all residents of the city.

From the same report, it appears "that for the forty-
six years previous to 1861, comprising the masterships
of Gould, Leverett, Dillaway, Dixwell, and Gardner
for ten years, the average number fitted for College
was 12.56 per annum."

The report then asks, "Do not these figures show
how eminently useful the Latin School has been in its
highest vocation,—the production of classical scholars?
During the last forty-six years, nearly six hundred young
men from this school have been admitted to honorable
standing in the several Universities and Colleges in
New England.

Such is the claim of Dr. Shurtleff, in behalf of the Latin School of Boston, upon the sympathy and support of a city, the largest, the most populous, and the wealthiest in New England. She may justly be proud of this, the oldest Grammar School of the land, as the richest gem in her crown of honor as the Athens of America, the home of noble scholars and princely merchants. Let her sustain this school, for she can well afford it, as a part of her system of public instruction, so often a matter of boast as the best in the United States, although from that system only seven and seven-tenths per annum of the graduating class of college candidates are received from the far-famed Public Schools of Boston. And yet this result, though put forth to the world by the Boston school committee as a matter of boasting, will be received with surprise as very small for a city whose population in 1861 was nearly 178,000, whose valuation for 1860 was $312,000,000, in whose Public Schools there were 28,000 pupils in 1861, of which only one pupil in 3,636 was fitted for "ye universitie" in one year, in conformity with the ancient statutes.

Compare now, with this record, the results of classical training in the number of candidates for College annually sent forth from Phillips Academy at Andover.

We have only the statistics for the last twenty-eight years, the period of Dr. S. H. Taylor's preceptorship. We make no estimate of Dr. Pierson's administration, or his successors, Mark Newman, John Adams, Osgood Johnson, and others, who were at the head of the school for the sixty years previous to Dr. Taylor's accession. We refer not to the results of the English school always sustained at Phillips Academy, at which Wm. H. Wells and J. S. Eaton have been masters, nor to the Normal Seminary connected with Phillips Academy for many years, the first established in America. We refer only to the department of the classics from which, in the last ten years, 46.9 per annum have been fitted for College. In the previous eighteen years, the average number fitted was 25⅔, and for the entire period of twenty-eight years, the average has been 33¼ per annum. This number does not include two hundred who advanced as far in their course of study as through the first or second term (three in a year) of the last year's course of study, more than half of whom were pretty nearly fitted for Colleges and others within two terms of study.

Thus, more than one thousand young men have been sent from Andover to the different Colleges, in a little more than a quarter of a century, by one eminent instructor. This one fact is enough to show the vitality of this institution as a power in the land. But the endowment on which all the departments of Phillips Academy rest as their basis, does not exceed $75,000, while the funds at Exeter do not vary much from $100,000.

But in these days, all the Colleges and nearly all Academies are no less schools of science than of the classics. All the best Colleges have scientific departments, and the Academies having the greatest patronage are furnished with instruction and apparatus for the preparation of young men for the higher scientific institutions. So extensive has the routine of scientific studies become, that they cannot be pursued with profit unless in well-endowed institutions where a course of study is established and adhered to. Hence, in Williston Seminary, the amplest provision is made for this branch of studies, as well as the classical department. As these branches cannot be well taught without special teachers and expensive cabinets and apparatus of every kind, the best Academies have been furnished with facilities of teaching in these respects as the High Schools with few exceptions have not been.

But the Public Schools have endeavored not only to provide classical but scientific instruction also, in obedience to a popular demand for a class of studies deemed specially practical; and the consequence has been, that in many places the Public Schools have been overburdened with an excess of branches of study, while the branches essential as the foundation of real mental culture have been discarded. This course has diminished the real value of the Public Schools, which have thus been made subservient to the wants of a few, while the essential interests of the many are disregarded.

The attempt has been made to accomplish too *high* things in what are called High Schools. Not only is it proposed to fit boys for "ye universitie," without regard to the question whether they wish to be fitted or not, but to teach the outlines of nearly all the branches for each one of which a professorship is deemed a necessity in a decent College. But this is an impossibility, even in the best High Schools of our largest cities and towns, without ignoring the grand idea of what ought to be, if it is not, the policy of the local High Schools everywhere, that they are supplementary to the Common Schools, and are high in relation to them, and not in relation to the Universities; and that they should not therefore be considered, except in rare instances, as taking the place which middle schools must occupy as intermediate between the highest local schools and the Colleges, which is the proper sphere and function of the academical system.

The progress of popular education, so called, does not consist (as it is so often falsely assumed to consist) in introducing *high* studies, and a great many of them, into a school having only one or two teachers, and thus make it *high*. For no progress is so sure as this to make a school the lowest of the low, in all the essential uses and qualities of education. The old staples of instruction (reading, writing, and arithmetic and grammar) cannot be dispensed with in the popular schools; for their uses are grounded in the absolutely necessary wants of the youthful mind. Any system, then, which substitutes other studies for these, is one whose whole tendency is to deteriorate, not to elevate, the quality of education. We are not sure but that Latin may take the place of English grammar to some extent in the Public Schools, but it must be solely as a disciplinary study to teach general grammar, and not with a view to a full classical course in the local schools of any grade of excellence. Indeed, we are not sure but that English grammar had better be discarded entirely, if in the course of Common School instruction it must be limited to only one or two terms, and then set aside as *finished*. And yet the text-books in that branch are as—

> Thick as autumnal leaves that strew the brooks
> In Valombrosa;

though they were all unwritten until late in the eighteenth century, when the countless progeny began to be.

How the literature of the Elizabethan age and Queen Anne's time, when Addison and his peers wrote the Spectator, could have existed, when such a branch as English grammar was unknown in any English or Grammar School, is a mystery for some modern Common School superintendent to solve. In this country arithmetic was taught in all the Common Schools without a text-book till after the Revolution, and geography was a study high enough to be a branch of College education; and yet these were the schools in which Washington and Franklin received all their elementary training. They were taught in schoolhouses not decent enough for an Irish shanty now, and yet Franklin, thus "fitted" for his calling, became such a master in philosophy and civil affairs as that he held the lightnings in his grasp and hurled tyrants from their thrones. How could he do all this, when in no Grammar School on earth had the merest elements of the natural sciences even been heard of? And yet he did not underrate the Grammar Schools of his native city, or decry, as modern sciolists do, the value of classical learning, or establish Franklin medals for some school of practical and naturalistic studies, to the detriment and discouragement of so-called *dead* languages and *dry* and "uninteresting" branches of study.

But the grand argument against the academical system of middle schools and against Colleges as well is, that pupils must not be domiciliated away from the supervision of parents and placed under the entire supervision of tutorial governors and teachers. It is assumed that there is "no place like home" for the higher gradations of mental culture as well as the lower. If all homes were places for intellectual development as good as we might conceive them to be, where the parents were themselves qualified in the best manner for the work of instruction and moral discipline, then it were well that home influences should predominate in every stage of intellectual growth. But the homes of the best and most learned men are not found to be thus adapted to the purposes of education. They lack both the power to advise and direct in respect to the best methods, especially in all the higher departments of learning. Even if well-educated parents understand the value of learning, they may yet be ignorant of its processes and best methods, even while they enjoy its uses. Hence it is that liberally educated men, more than others, seek the best seats of learning for the education of their own children. They understand, as others do not, how that the local influences of home often tend to neutralize the best benefits, which the formative or transformative power of a College or Academy exerts on a young and wayward mind. Nor does the argument hold any better, though often urged, that the Public School system is any more in sympathy with the genius of our democratic institutions than the academical system in its middle or higher grades.

We do not deny that the Public School tends strongly to modify and remove those social distinctions, which it is the direct aim of home training, in many instances, to create and intensify. The boy of Beacon Street may recite his lesson in the Boston Latin School on the same seat with the boy of North Street; but the good influences of the morning session of each day, in obliterating factitious distinctions and creating good-fellowship, may not last longer than the dinner-hour, when all the power of home associations resumes its undiminished sway. It is not so in those schools, where the pupils come together from localities remote from each other, and from under the influence of social customs and notions most unlike. Here nothing is more common than to see the rich and the poor domiciliate together on grounds of perfect reciprocity, and forming the strongest fellowships in spite of antecedents of birth and position most diverse. If there can be found on earth a realization of that dream of politicians, a republic where there is a perfect equality of rights and privileges, and a perfect reciprocity of sympathy and social fellowship, independent absolutely of the distinctions of the outside world, that realization is a community of students in an American Academy or College.

In the home or local system of schools, the aim is really private education, and for ends more or less personal, though it be obtained at the public expense. In the academical or collegiate system of schools, the aim is a true public education, though it may be obtained by means legally private; that is, such as furnished by individuals or corporations.

The local system respects the parental will and dignity on the ground that, as parents, in their individual or social capacity, pay for the tuition of their children and appoint the teacher, they have a right to control all the methods and processes and influences of instruction; that is, they may say what shall and what shall not be taught. Such a policy as this, for the period of childhood during the time of rudimental training, is obviously the very best for the vast majority of pupils, since, during the earliest stages of education, the parents, who are the natural protectors of their children, are generally competent to act for them in respect to their intellectual as well as their physical wants. As the great majority of the young can never go much beyond the rudiments of all useful learning, the Public School system is most obviously founded in the eternal verities of things. But the period of childhood and the training proper for that period has its natural range and limits, and these limits and the course proper for those limits cannot be essentially changed, so as to substitute therefor the studies and the discipline of maturer years. This principle will not fail to be regarded, if the idea of adolescence and full majority is admitted, which idea some educators seem to disregard, as do the Chinese and some parents nominally Christian also, since in their system of training the child is never of age till the parent dies, and not even then.

The recognition of the period of adolescence, in a system of education, demands a grade of schools in which the interest of the pupil in his own welfare is a consideration paramount to the parental will or dignity; and hence, although the parent may rightly control the course of the pupil so far as to direct the place of his education, yet, while in that place, the teacher stands in all respects *in loco parentis,* and the parent in all that pertains to the appropriate work of instruction and discipline never stands *in loco docentis.*

It is evident, therefore, that as the period of adolescence draws to its close, the aim of school training must more and more have a direct reference to the welfare of the pupil as the party mainly concerned; and less and less to that of the parent, except, indeed, so far as that, by sympathy and affection, he may regard the welfare of his child, at all times, as his own. But in the later stages of education, at the higher seminaries, the authority of home cannot predominate in opposition to the teacher's labor and influence. The students must be held in subjection by a power stronger than that of any home influence can ordinarily be. Such a power a vigorous seat of learning affords, and it meets the wants of subjective training at the period when its force is most efficient and most needed—

To curb the fiery heart of youth.

Such a power was exerted by Arnold at Rugby, and by Dr. Whewell, the Master of Trinity at Cambridge, recently deceased. Such a power have many teachers, both among the living and the dead, exercised in the Academic Schools of our own land,—a power which must forever make our Academies and Colleges indispensable, since they supply those forces of strength which no family, or hamlet, or town, or city can furnish without their aid.

Every college graduate can understand, as others cannot, the peculiar advantages of mental development and of those executive qualities of the manly character, which come as the incidental results of a public education, and which the training of home or of any local school, however excellent it may be in other respects, rarely confers.

Hence the necessity of a public education for places of public service and for all kinds of civil and ecclesiastical duties, which require men of "large discourse" or liberal and comprehensive culture. Hence the necessity of Colleges and Universities, and hence, too, the need of having institutions which shall, in all their forces of moral and intellectual power, keep pace with the wants of our advancing American civilization, ultimately to be, in its maturity, the noblest in the world's history. We shall need Universities as much better than Oxford and Cambridge, as the destiny of American society is to be better and more powerful than that of England or any of the continental kingdoms and empires.

But as preliminary to their ultimate enlargement, and as a condition of their efficiency even in their present form, we need a system of middle schools having the same great ends of social advancement in view, and tending to the same results, which it is the object of our highest seminaries to accomplish.

The Universities of England and the Continent of Europe have for ages received all their annual accessions from the middle schools, in which the foundations of all sound education and training have been laid, the quality and degrees of which have been determined by the wisest of men, who have fully understood its uses as well as its processes and instruments. And the education obtained in the "great Public Schools" of England has exceeded, in the extent and value of classical training, that which the best American Colleges have furnished until within a recent period.

But the day has come when the Colleges of this country must embrace within their curriculum other studies than the elemental studies of a classical or scientific course. Four years are too few to include the multitude of studies which a general course of liberal culture must embrace as the limit of graduation. And a great share of the classical and mathematical studies of the first two years of the college course, as now arranged, could be better attended to in middle schools, under good teachers and with proper endowments and accommodations. The temptations to dissipation would be far less, and the standard of attainments far greater in studies, which, though pursued in the College, are really and altogether elemental, when the rank of scholarship in the English and European Universities is considered.

So the middle schools are more desirable places than the College to lay the foundations of not scholarship only, but of the highest qualities of manly character. Dr. Arnold's influence was such as to shield his pupils with a moral panoply of protection against the folly and dissoluteness of university life, the occasion of utter ruin to so many young men in all the high seats of learning.

There is need, then, not only of the continued existence of the best Academies of New England, but of their great enlargement and improvement. They are needed to supply that lack of the best culture which the local schools of the rural sections of the country can never supply. They are needed as places of resort for training the best minds of both the city and country under certain influences, which few purely local schools can have under the best of circumstances. They are needed to prepare for the Colleges the best material to make good scholarship, much of which is found among the hill towns of New England, though they may be as rough as Mount Helicon, on whose slopes the muses did not deign the less to dwell because they were wild and barren.

We need them, that the proper work of all the local schools, both of the city and country, may not be interfered with, in the vain attempt to make them answer for uses and purposes not belonging to their proper design, in educating the whole mass of the popular mind to the highest possible average of attainment at the public expense. The duty of sustaining the local schools, in all their grades, will be met by the American people, and the local schools will have attained their limit of perfection, not when they shall attempt to fit one out of a thousand boys, as he ought to be to enter College, but to educate the nine hundred and ninety-nine, who cannot and ought not to go to College, in the best possible manner, for, not the learned professions, but for the not less honorable callings, which society demands shall be filled by well-educated and good citizens. It is perhaps enough that the State confine itself to this great work, the education of the people, by improving to their utmost capacity the local schools of every grade.

With respect to Colleges and middle schools, it is perhaps all that we can expect, if we demand the kindly regard of the State and such scanty appropriations as can be afforded. For the history of the higher education of society shows, that, in all ages of modern civilization, at least, Universities and classical schools have had to depend on the enlightened liberality of a few noble and generous benefactors. All the Colleges and Universities of

England and the Continent, all the Colleges of this country, the oldest and the youngest, all the important Academies and professional schools, are monuments of *private* liberality, supported chiefly by the endowments of those who, blessed by Providence with wealth, have left it, as a legacy of perennial good, for the successive generations of men, who, as they receive the benefit of their benefactions, will revere and bless their memory with "perpetual benedictions."

4. Opposition to the Academies

As early as the 1820's, objections were raised against the private nature of the academies. James G. Carter, in one of his well-known letters to the Hon. William Prescott, pressed this issue forcefully in 1824. Three decades later, George S. Boutwell, who succeeded Horace Mann as secretary to the Massachusetts Board of Education, took up the same cudgel. The arguments advanced in other states were similar to those of the Massachusetts leaders, if somewhat less eloquent.

James G. Carter:
To the Hon. William Prescott*
(1824)

. . . The next in order from the primary schools *were* the *grammar schools,* properly so called. These were established by the law of 1789, in all towns containing two hundred families. The object and the tendency of these higher schools were, to raise the standard of instruction, and elicit talents and genius wherever they might be found. Many through the medium of these schools have found their way to the University, and become distinguished in society, who might otherwise never have known their own powers, or thought it possible to aspire to the advantages of a public education. But this part of the system has never received that attention, which its importance demands. It has always been viewed with prejudice, and been thought to be an institution for the accommodation of a few, at the expense of the many. In many places, for want of a thorough knowledge of the subject, those for whose particular advantage the grammar schools were intended, have been most opposed to their support. The law, therefore, has been borne with impatience,—has been explained away and evaded,—till

* James G. Carter, *Letters to the Hon. William Prescott, LL.D. on the Free Schools of New England, with Remarks upon the Principles of Instruction* (Boston, 1824), pp. 32–47. The selection is from Letter III.

at length, the prejudice has been sent into the legislature, and the whole provision is struck out of the statute book. At least, the remnant which remains can be of no possible use for the encouragement of the schools. All towns in the Commonwealth are now excused from supporting grammar schools, except five or six of the most populous. And these are precisely the towns, which least need legislative interference. A law of the legislature to oblige Boston, for example, to make appropriations for schools, is preposterous, when that city already expends upon the education of its children and youth, nearly as much as the whole remaining state. But during the series of years, while the grammar schools have been neglected, the friends of the free schools have had an appeal to those liberal and enlightened minds, which could better foresee the happy effects of a different policy. And this appeal has never been made in vain. Whenever the public interest in schools has declined or been diverted, by the various necessities, which press upon a people, in a comparatively new country, it has soon been roused again, and stimulated in the proper direction. If appropriations have not been so liberal as might be wished, those have always been found, who would encourage the cause by endowments for schools of a higher order. These schools or academies, as they are more frequently called, have been generally founded by individuals, and afterwards made corporations with grants of land or money from the State authorities. They have now become very numerous throughout New England. In Massachusetts, they are found in every county, and oftentimes within ten or fifteen miles of each other. They have generally been made a class above the *grammar schools*. Here, young men are prepared for teachers in the primary schools,—for mercantile life,—or for the University. This class of schools is not entirely free. The instructer is supported in part by the proceeds of funds, which have arisen from private or public munificence; and in part, by a tax on each scholar. For the rich and those in easy circumstances, these schools answer the same, and probably a better purpose, than the grammar schools, contemplated by the late law; but they are out of the reach of the poor. Many a poor and industrious man would spare the labour of his son, and give him an opportunity to learn, perhaps to fit for college, while the means were in his own town, who could but ill afford a considerable tax for tuition, and the price of board in a neighbouring town. This will be the effect of the repeal of the school law. The rich, at a little more expense to be sure, but that is of no consequence with them, will patronize and improve the condition of the academies for their own accommodation; while the poor will be left with no advantages above the primary schools. One avenue, and that a broad and easy one for the progress of genius in humble life, is now shut on a large proportion of the community; and talents,

>Th' applause of listening senates to command,

are doomed to a virtual death by the operation of this measure. Its effects are the more to be dreaded, because they will follow their cause slowly, and be felt most at some distant period, when it will be most difficult to trace the evil to its source. The means of education, though the most powerful instrument, by which a government may effect the character of the people, are not an instrument, by which they can produce an immediate result. As the good to be expected from liberal appropriations, though sure to follow, is realized to the country, only at a distance from the outfit; so the evils of withholding encouragement, though as sure to follow, are still at a distance. But happy experience ought to have taught *this community*, how to estimate the magnitude of the good and evil of the different policies, even though they are at a distance. We are now in the possession and enjoyment of those advantages for education, purchased by the sacrifices of our ancestors. And the question in regard to appropriations at the present day, is, whether we shall transmit those advantages unimpaired to posterity; or whether we shall shut our eyes on the future, and suffer the animating and vivifying principle of our free government to be extinguished by neglect, or perverted by a heedless and inefficient encouragement. We all profess the deepest veneration for the character of the pilgrims, and those characters, who laid the foundation of our free government; and can we consistently depart from those traits in their policy, which have made them venerable, and our government free? To praise the institutions and happy state of our country, and to congratulate ourselves on the free enjoyment of them, is not so much to praise ourselves, as it is to praise the liberal and enlightened policy of those, by whose wisdom and foresight we have inherited such privileges and happiness. Posterity will judge of our policy, at some future period, by its effects on *their* condition, as we now judge of the policy of our ancestors, by its effects on *our* condition. If we compare the encouragement afforded to schools and seminaries of learning, by the pilgrims of Plymouth and New England, with their resources; and then in connexion, compare the encouragement afforded them at the present day, with our resources; we shall be astonished and disgusted with our niggardly and parsimonious policy. We seem to rely entirely upon the liberality and munificence of indi-

viduals to redeem our degeneracy in this respect. What
would our ancestors have thought of their posterity,
those ancestors, who nearly two hundred years since,
amidst all the embarrassments of a new settlement, provided by law for the support of *grammar schools in all
towns of one hundred families, "the master thereof being
able to instruct youth so far as they may be fitted for the
University?"* or what would our fathers have thought of
their children, those fathers who, in 1780, enjoined it in
their *constitution,* upon *"the Legislatures and Magis-
trates, in all future periods of this Commonwealth, to
cherish the interests of literature and the sciences, and
all seminaries of them; especially the University at
Cambridge, public schools, and* GRAMMAR SCHOOLS *in the
towns;"* if they could have foreseen, that after one relax-
ation and another, in forty years, those children would
so far forget their duty to "cherish the GRAMMAR
SCHOOLS," as to strike them out of existence? What the
peculiar condition of the people of this State is, which
renders the support of this class of schools unnecessary,
impolitick, or unjust, I have never been able to understand. And, although I have been at some pains on the
subject, I have never yet learned, what the arguments
were, which carried the repeal of the law through the
last General Court. Arguments there must have been,
and strong ones, or such an alarming innovation would
never have been suffered, upon an institution, to which
the people, till quite lately, have always expressed the
strongest attachment. Was that class of schools considered
unnecessary? If so, what has made them unnecessary?
Either the people have no longer need to receive the
kind of instruction, those schools were intended to afford;
or they must receive the same instruction in some other
way. The policy, and in our government, the necessity

of eliciting the talents of the country, by every possible means, will be demonstrated, when we consider how many of our most distinguished Jurists, Statesmen, and Divines, have received their early instruction in the primary and grammar schools of some obscure country village. None, I believe, can be found, who will say, the people have no longer *need* of such facilities, for bringing forward to notice the promising talents of their children, and of giving to our country some of its greatest benefactors. Then by abolishing the grammar schools, it is expected the people will receive the same instruction in some other way. But two possible sources occur, which promise in any degree to supply the chasm in the system. The primary schools on the one hand,—and the academies on the other. Neither of these sources will answer the expectation, or be adequate to the purpose. The primary schools will not come up to the necessary standard, either as they are contemplated by the law, or as they are, and promise to be, supported by the people. And the academies are out of the reach of precisely that class of people, who most need the encouragement offered by the late grammar schools. The effect of the repeal of the law upon the primary schools, is as yet, but matter of conjecture. It is probably expected by some, and it is certainly to be hoped by all, that striking from the system the class of schools immediately above them, they will be improved so as in some degree to supply the place of the higher schools. If this expectation had any foundation, or if there were any probability, it would be realized in some good degree, it would not be so much a matter of regret, that the late measure was adopted. But several reasons induce me to believe, that the expectation is altogether visionary; and that the measure will have a tendency to sink, rather than improve the condition of the primary schools. Although the late law has not been executed for some years upon a very liberal construction, yet the knowledge, that it existed, had some effect, to raise the character of instructers in the lower schools. To benefit the schools, all possible motives should be offered to raise the qualifications of the teachers. The repeal of the law has removed the strongest barrier to prevent the obtrusions of ignorance. Experience has long since proved, that the approbation of the selectmen as to the character, and of the minister as to the literary qualifications, is no sufficient check, upon the pretensions of incompetent instructers. Those, who aspire to the place of teachers in the primary schools, are very frequently found in the families of the very men, whose approbation is required. And however vigilant and candid they may intend to be, in the discharge of their duty in this respect, paternal affection is a most deceitful medium, through which a father looks upon the merits of his son. And the condition of the clergy, in the country, particularly at the present day, is not such as would allow us to expect from them, a very positive and decided veto in such matters, upon the pleasure of the principal inhabitants of their towns. We have now no checks, but the very inefficient one above described, to prevent the employment of incompetent instructers. And since the interest and influence of the candidate for such employment, as well as the interest and influence of his friends, will always be upon the wrong side; it is much to be feared, that the mass of instructers, in the primary schools, will receive no other opportunities for improvement, than are afforded in the very schools, where they commence teaching. If this view of the subject is correct, the strong tendency of the present arrangement must be, to sink the condition of the primary schools. And the only, or at least, the greatest counteracting influence, which has existed heretofore, is removed, by abolishing the late grammar schools. Few towns have supported a grammar school the whole continued year, at one place. They have employed several instructers, *qualified as the law directed,* and by opening several schools of this kind at the same time, have made up the amount of a year, all perhaps, during the winter months. This evasion, which was a very general one in those towns, which took the trouble to evade at all, you will perceive, was virtually putting the grammar school-masters into the primary schools. The consequence has been what we should expect. Although the grammar schools have in many places disappeared in form and name, yet the people have a tolerable equivalent, in the vastly improved condition of the primary schools. Even those, who have commenced teachers from some of these schools, have possessed all the advantage of the grammar schools, intended by the law. The existence of the law, therefore, even with so very inefficient an execution of it, has had the direct tendency to improve the condition of those schools, in which grammar masters have been employed; and an indirect influence on the other schools, by better qualifying those who have and will commence teachers, with no advantages above those afforded in the common schools.

The repeal of the law obviates the necessity of the evasion, which I have described as operating so favourably upon the primary schools. And as the qualifications of the instructers are diminished, the character of the schools must decline. To this, probably, all will readily assent. But it may, perhaps, be said, the qualifications of the instructers are as high, for all practical and useful purposes, as they were under the former law, as it was executed. In the first place, it is not fair or just to reason from the law as it *was executed,* rather than as it *should have been* executed. In the next place, allowing ourselves so to reason, we shall not, I believe, arrive at the same result. The qualifications of the grammar schoolmasters, were, that they should be "of good morals, well instructed in the *Latin, Greek,* and English languages." This class of schools is now abolished, and *"Geography"* is added to the former qualifications of the teachers of primary schools. Allowing the two classes of schools to have been perfectly amalgamated, which is a great concession in point of fact, as well as acknowledging a great perversion of the law; we have dispensed with Latin and Greek, and require Geography in their stead. I have no desire to lessen the estimation, in which geography is held as a study peculiarly adapted to our primary schools. And I am ready to concede, that probably ten will wish to study geography, where one would wish to study Latin and Greek. Now, if an instructer, who is qualified to teach Latin and Greek, could not by any possibility be qualified, at the same time, to teach Geography, and all the minor studies of our schools, I should consider myself as having conceded the whole argument. But this is not the fact. These qualifications are so far from being incompatible, that they *generally* exist in a superior degree in connexion with each other. The connexion, to be sure, is not so essential, that a man may not be a very good teacher of Latin and Greek, and still know very little of any thing else. Still as the studies are arranged in all our schools, academies, and colleges, where young men are prepared for teachers, all the elementary studies, including geography, are generally taught before the languages. So that by adding them to the qualifications, even if it were *never* required of the instructers to teach them, we ensure more mature and accomplished scholars in those branches, which are more frequently and generally taught. I would not be understood to discuss, much less to approve this arrangement of studies, for those destined to be scholars by profession. Such arrangement exists, and I avail myself of the fact for my present purpose. But besides ensuring better teachers for the common branches, there are always some, who would attend to the languages, as preparatory to a publick education, if they had opportunity. And if affording the opportunity to all of every town, should be the means of drawing out but few of superiour talents, even those few are worthy of the highest consideration and regard from the publick, who possess them. These and similar considerations, which I cannot here state, have convinced me, I know not whether they will convince any one else, that the repeal of the grammar school law, even if we could never hope it would be executed upon a more liberal construction, than it has been for the last ten years, will have a direct tendency to sink the condition and prospects of the primary schools.

There is one other point of view, in which the effect of the measure will be equally pernicious and equally certain. I mean its effect upon the *manners* of the scholars. This was a consideration deemed so important as to be provided for in the law of 1789. In proportion as the qualifications of instructers are lessened, it becomes easy for those to commence teachers, who have had no advantages above the primary schools. And although good manners, or "decent behaviour" have no *essential* connexion with the other accomplishments, or Latin and Greek in particular, yet they are by no means incompatible. And those, who have had the advantages of the higher schools, academies, or colleges, will be more likely to have acquired some refinement of manners, than those, who begin to teach without any preparation, except in the very place, where they have themselves been taught.

In publick and large seminaries of learning, which bring together young men from different towns, states, and sections of the country, the change in habits, manners, and feelings towards each other, is astonishingly rapid. They come together with feelings and prejudices, and oftentimes with a dialect peculiar to the different places, from which they come, and each staring and wondering at the excessive *strangeness* of the other. But a very short time loosens their local prejudices, and teaches them, that all excellence is not peculiar to any one place. The whole exterior and deportment of the young man is often almost entirely transformed, in the short space of a few weeks. The change and improvement in this respect are more rapid at first, and quite as important and valuable to him, as his acquisitions in knowledge. What has a more direct tendency to improve "the manners" and deportment of the children, who attend our schools, than to observe some refinement in their instructer? Such is the personal influence of an instructer in a common school, that whether he is refined or vulgar, or whether he attends to the manners of his pupils or not, his manners will infallibly be imitated and copied by all, for the time, as a model of perfection. The different sections of our country are more free from dialects of the same language than any other in the world. What has produced this uniformity of language, so desirable on every consideration, but our public and common seminaries of learning,—the frequent and intimate commercial and literary intercourse between different parts of the country,—and the numerous points of contact between the educated and uneducated parts of the community? For the interest and happiness of the whole, and especially, the lower and uneducated classes of the community, it is certainly desirable these points of contact and intercourse should be multiplied, rather than diminished. For these reasons, the employment of instructers in our schools, who have had the advantages of some publick school or college, is an object of great consideration. Besides being the most direct and effectual means, of inculcating "decent behaviour,"—of reconciling the prejudices of different parts of the country, and different classes of the community; there is still another point of view, in which the measure is not less important. It tends more than any thing else, to lessen the distance and weaken the jealousies, which very generally subsist between the educated and uneducated. The talents and acquirements of a young man of publick education are often lost to the unlettered community for some years, while they have a delicious season of mutually hating and despising each other. These evils are in some degree obviated, when, by the kind of intercourse usually subsisting between a *publick* instructer and the *publick,* they are taught by experience their mutual worth and dependence as members of the same body politick.

As the Academies are not entirely free schools, we cannot calculate upon *them* to supply instruction to the mass of the people. These are most respectable establishments, and some of them are hardly inferior in the advantages, they afford for acquiring a thorough education, to some institutions, which are dignified with the name of colleges. It is not desirable, that their condition should be impaired. Nor need any fears be entertained, that their condition will be impaired. There are enough in the community, who duly estimate the advantages of a good education, and who are able to sustain the expense of these schools, to ensure their permanent support. And as the other classes of schools, which are free, are annihilated or decline in their character and condition, the academies will be encouraged by those, who can better appreciate the advantages of good schools, and better afford the necessary expense. So far as it regards the accommodation and pecuniary interest of the rich, and those of moderate property, it is matter of indifference, whether the legislature or publick make any appropriations or provisions for schools or not. They can and will take care for themselves. These are not the classes of the community to suffer, when government withhold encouragement from the schools. It is the poor, who are to suffer. They must educate their children in *free* schools, and in their own neighborhood, or not educate them at all. The expense of tuition, of books, and of board at the academies are so appalling, as to put the advantages of those schools quite beyond the power of a vast proportion of the community. In the towns where academies happen to be fixed, the poor will of course derive some increased advantages; but these towns are so few compared with the whole, and the incident expenses for books and tuition are so considerable, that for all purposes of directly and efficiently educating the whole mass of the people, the academies may be left out of calculation. For not one in twenty, if one in fifty, throughout the State, will ever find their way to any of them.

George S. Boutwell:
"The Relative Merits of Public
High Schools and Endowed Academies"*
(1857)

The distinguishing difference between the advocates of
endowed schools and of free schools is this: those who
advocate the system of endowed academies go back in
their arguments to one foundation, which is, that in education of the higher grades the great mass of the people
are not to be trusted. And those who advocate a system
of free education in high schools put the matter where
we have put the rights of property and liberty, where we
put the institutions of law and religion—upon the public
judgment. And we will stand there. If the public will not
maintain institutions of learning, then, I say, let institutions of learning go down. If I belong to a state which
cannot be moved from its extremities to its centre, and
from its centre to its extremities, for the maintenance of
a system of public instruction, then, in that respect, I
disown that state; and if there be one state in this Union
whose people cannot be aroused to maintain a system of
public instruction, then they are false to the great leading

* George S. Boutwell, *Thoughts on Educational Topics and Institutions* (Boston, 1859), pp. 152–163. This essay was first delivered
as an address before the American Institute of Instruction in
1857.

idea of American principles, and of civil, political, and religious liberty.

It is easy to enumerate the advantages of a system of public education, and the evils—I say evils—of endowed academies, whether free or charging payment for tuition. Endowed academies are not, in all respects, under all circumstances, and everywhere, to be condemned. In discussing this subject, it may be well for me to state the view that I have of the proper position of endowed academies. They have a place in the educational wants of this age. This is especially true of academies of the highest rank, which furnish an elevated and extended course of instruction. To such I make no objection, but I would honor and encourage them. Yet I regard private schools, which do the work usually done in public schools, as temporary, their necessity as ephemeral, and I think that under a proper public sentiment they will soon pass away. They cannot stand,—such has been the experience in Massachusetts,—they cannot stand by the side of a good system of public education. Yet where the population is sparse, where there is not property sufficient to enable the people to establish a high school, then an endowed school may properly come in to make up the deficiency, to supply the means of education to which the public wealth, at the present moment, is unequal. Endowed institutions very properly, also, give a professional education to the people. At this moment we cannot look to the public to give that education which is purely professional. But what we do look to the public for is this: to furnish the means of education to the children of the whole people, without any reference to social, pecuniary, political, or religious distinctions, so that every person may have a preliminary education sufficient for the ordinary business of life.

It is said that the means of education are better in an endowed academy, or in an endowed free school, than they can be in a public school. What is meant by *means* of education? I understand that, first and chiefly, as extraneous means of education, we must look to a correct public sentiment, which shall animate and influence the teacher, which shall give direction to the school, which shall furnish the necessary public funds. An endowed free academy can have none of these things permanently. Take, for example, the free school established at Norwich by the liberality of thirty or forty gentlemen, who contributed ninety thousand dollars. What security is there that fifty years hence, when the educational wants of the people shall be changed, when the population of Norwich shall be double or treble what it is now, when science shall make greater demands, when these forty contributors shall have passed away, this institution will answer the wants of that generation? According to what we know of the history of this country, it will be entirely inadequate; and, though none of us may live to see the prediction fulfilled or falsified, I do not hesitate to say that the school will ultimately prove a failure, because it is founded in a mistake.

Then look and see what would have been the state of things if there had been public spirit invoked to establish a public high school, and if the means for its support had been raised by taxation of all the people, so that the system of education would have expanded according to the growth of the city, and year by year would have accommodated itself to the public wants and public zeal in the cause. Though these means seem now to be ample, they will by and by be found too limited. The school at Norwich is encumbered with regulations; and so every endowed institution is likely to be, because the right of a man to appropriate his property to a particular object carries with it, in the principles of common law, and in the administration of the law, in all free governments, the right to declare, to a certain extent, how that property shall be applied. Rules have been established— very proper and judicious rules for today. But who knows that a hundred years hence they will be proper or acceptable at all? They have also established a board of trustees, ultimately to be reduced to twenty-five. These trustees have power to perpetuate themselves. Who does not see that you have severed this institution from the public sentiment of the city of Norwich, and that ultimately that city will seek for itself what it needs; and that, a hundred years hence, it will not consent to live, in the civilization of that time, under the regulations which forty men have now established, however wise the regulations may at the present moment be?

One hundred and fifty years ago, Thomas Hollis, of London, made a bequest to the university at Cambridge, with a provision that on every Thursday a professor should sit in his chair to answer questions in polemic theology. All well enough then; but the public sentiment of to-day will not carry it out.

So it may be with the school at Norwich a hundred years hence. The man or state that sacrifices the living public judgment to the opinion of a dead man, or a dead generation, makes a great mistake. We should never substitute, beyond the power of revisal, the opinion of a past generation for the opinion of a living generation. I trust to the living men of to-day as to what is necessary to meet our existing wants, rather than to the wisest men who lived in Greece or Rome. And, if I would not trust the wise men of Greece and Rome, I do not know why the people, a hundred years hence, should trust the wise men of our own time.

And then look further, and see how, under a system of public instruction, you can build up, from year to year, in the growth of the child, a system according to his wants. Private instruction cannot do this. What do we do where we have a correct system? A child goes into a primary school. He is not to go out when he attains a certain age. He might as well go out when he is of a certain height; there would be as much merit in one case as in the other. But he is advanced when he has made adequate attainments. Who does not see that the child is incited and encouraged and stimulated by every sentiment to which you should appeal? And, then, when he has gone up to the grammar school, we say to him, "You are to go into the high school when you have made certain attainments." And who is to judge of these attainments? A committee appointed by the people, over whom the people have some ultimate control. And in that control they have security for two things: first, that the committee shall not be suspected of partiality; and secondly, that they shall not be actually guilty of partiality. In the same manner, there is security for the proper connection between the high school and the schools below. But in the school at Norwich—of which I speak because it is now prominent—you have a board of twenty-five men, irresponsible to the people. They select a committee of nine; that committee determines what candidates shall be transferred from the grammar schools to the high school. May there not be suspicion of partiality? If a boy or girl is rejected, you look for some social, political, or religious influence which has caused the rejection, and the parent and child complain. Here is a great evil; for the real and apparent justice of the examination and decision by which pupils are transferred from one school to another is vital to the success of the system.

There is another advantage in the system of public

high schools, which I imagine the people do not always
at first appreciate. It is, that the private school, with the
same teachers, the same apparatus, and the same means,
cannot give the education which may be, and usually is,
furnished in the public schools. This statement may seem
to require some considerable support. We must look at
facts as they are. Some people are poor; I am sorry for
them. Some people are rich, and I congratulate them
upon their good fortune. But it is not so much of a benefit, after all, as many think. It is worth something in this
world, no doubt, to be rich; but what is the result of that
condition upon the family first, the school afterwards,
and society finally? It is, that some learn the lesson of
life a little earlier than others; and that lesson is the
lesson of self-reliance, which is worth more than—I will
not say a knowledge of the English language—but worth
more than Latin or Greek. If the great lesson of self-
reliance is to be learned, who is more likely to acquire it
early,—the child of the poor, or the child of the rich; the
child who has most done for him, or the child who is
under the necessity of doing most for himself? Plainly,
the latter. Now, while a system of public instruction in
itself cannot be magnified in its beneficial influences to
the poor and to the children of the poor, it is equally
beneficial to the rich in the facility it affords for the instruction of their children. Is it not worth something
to the rich man, who cannot, from the circumstances of
the case, teach self-reliance around the family hearth, to
send his child to school to learn this lesson with other
children, that he may be stimulated, that he may be pro-
voked to exertions which he would not otherwise have
made? For, be it remembered that in our schools public
sentiment is as well marked as in a college, or a town, or
a nation; that it moves forward in the same way. And

the great object of a teacher should be to create a public sentiment in favor of virtue. There should be some pioneers in favor of forming a correct public sentiment; and when it is formed it moves on irresistibly. It is like the river made up of drops from the mountain side, moving on with more and more power, until everything in its waters is carried to the destined end.

So in a public school. And it is worth much to the man of wealth that there may be, near his own door, an institution to which he may send his children, and under the influence of which they may be carried forward. For, depend upon it, after all we say about schools and institutions of learning, it is nevertheless true of education, as a statesman has said of the government, that the people look to the school for too much. It is not, after all, a great deal that the child gets there; but, if he only gets the ability to acquire more than he has, the schools accomplish something. If you give a child a little knowledge of geography or arithmetic, and have not developed the power to accomplish something for himself, he comes to but little in the world. But put him into the school,—the primary, grammar, and high school, where he must learn for himself,—and he will be fitted for the world of life into which he is to enter.

You will see in this statement that, with the same parties, the same means of education, the same teachers, the public schools will accomplish more than private schools.

I find everywhere, and especially in the able address of Mr. Gulliver, to which I have referred, that the public schools are treated as of questionable morality, and it is implied that something would be gained by removing certain children from the influence of these schools. If I were speaking from another point of view, very likely

I should feel bound to hold up the evils and defects which actually exist in public schools; but when I consider them in contrast with endowed and private schools, I do not hesitate to say that the public schools compare favorably; and, as the work of education goes on, the comparison will be more and more to their advantage. Why? I know something of the private institutions in Massachusetts; and there are boys in them who have left the public schools because they have fallen in their classes, and the public interest would not justify their continuance in the schools. It was always true that private schools did not represent the world exactly as it was. It is worth everything to a boy or girl, man or woman, to look the world in the face as it is.

Therefore, the public school, when it represents the world as it is, represents the facts of life. The private school never has done and never will do this; and as time goes on, it will be less and less a true representative of the world. From this point of view, it seems to be a mistake on the part of parents to exclude their children from the world. Is it not better that the child should learn something of society, even of its evils, when under your influence, and when you can control him by your counsel and example, than to permit him finally to go out, as you must when his majority comes, perhaps to be seduced in a moment, as it were, from his allegiance to virtue? Virtue is not exclusion from the presence of vice; but it is resistance to vice in its presence. And it is the duty of parents to provide safeguards for the support of their children against these temptations. When Cicero was called on to defend Muræna against the slander that, as he had lived in Asia, he had been guilty of certain crimes, and when the testimony failed to substantiate the charge, the orator said, "And if Asia does carry with it a suspicion of luxury, surely it is a praiseworthy thing, not never to have seen Asia, but to have lived temperately in Asia." And we have yet higher authority. It is not the glory of Christ, or of Christianity, that its Divine Author was without temptation, but that, being tempted, he was without sin. This is the great lesson of the day.

The duty of the public is to provide means for the education of all. To do that, we need the political, social, and moral power of all, to sustain teachers and institutions of learning; and endowed or free schools, depending upon the contributions of individuals, can never, in a free country, be raised to the character of a system. If you rob the public schools of the influence of our public-spirited men, if they take away a portion of their pupils from them, our system is impaired. It must stand as a whole, educating the entire people, and looking to all for support, or it cannot be permanently maintained.

5. Academy Life

The four following selections illustrate a variety of institutions. The circular of the academy for girls at Albany shows the breadth of the curriculum as well as its similarity to the course of studies commonly offered in the boys' academies. The major difference is that instruction in the classical languages was an "extra" in the girls' academy. Gould's Academy in Bethel, Maine, was a typical coeducational institution, with a college-preparatory ("language") course and an "English" course for those not planning to continue their studies. The fact that the curriculum is described in terms of texts provides an inkling of the probable pedagogy employed at the school. Gould's can be considered a thoroughly characteristic academy, and institutions like it were seen in all parts of the country.

The rules for teachers and students at the New Braunfels Academy in Texas provide some idea of the character of student life and the measure of freedom allowed the teachers. Again, such rules can be found for academies in widely separated regions.

Circular of the
Albany Female Academy*
(1836)

LOCATION.—This Institution is situated in North Pearl-street, between Maiden-Lane and Steuben-street.

A board of thirteen Trustees, elected annually by the stockholders, according to the provisions of the charter, have the general management of the affairs of the Academy.

SYSTEM OF INSTRUCTION.—The Institution is divided into six departments, exclusive of the classes composed of those scholars from each of the higher departments, who are pursuing the study of the French and Spanish Languages, Natural History, Chemistry, and Botany.

In the Sixth Department, the rudiments of education are commenced. The books used are, Worcester's Primer of the English Language, Gallaudet's Picture Defining and Reading Book, Webster's Spelling-Book, Barber's First Book on Elocution, Olney's Easy Reader, the New-Testament, Smith's Geography, Emerson's and Smith's Introductory Arithmetics. This department is furnished with Holbrook's apparatus for primary schools.

In the Fifth Department, regular instruction in writing commenced, Colburn's First Lessons and Smith's Geog-

* *Circular and Catalogue of the Albany Female Academy, 1836* (Albany, N.Y., 1836), pp. 2–5.

raphy, Hart's Geography, Smith's Intellectual and Practical Grammar, Irving's Catechisms of the History of Various Nations, Trimmer's Elements of Natural History, and Barber's First Book. As an exercise in the definition and use of words, and the structure of language, the pupils are daily required to incorporate in sentences, to be written by them, words given to them by their teachers.

In the Fourth Department, the studies of the fifth reviewed. The Malte Brun Geography and Atlas by Goodrich, Worcester's General History and Chart, History of N.Y., Gleig's Bible History, Biblical Literature and Chart, History of U. S., Smith's Productive Grammar and Parker's Composition. In this department, Smith's Arithmetic commenced; exercises in composition in the journal and letter form.

In each of these three departments is a library, carefully selected with reference to the capacities and attainments of the pupils, and to be used by them at intervals during the hours of study.

In the Third Department, Parker's Composition, and Smith's Arithmetic concluded, History of New-York, and the other studies of the fourth reviewed; Goodrich's History of the United States, with Emerson's Questions, Robbins' General History, History of England, Ancient Geography, Newman's Rhetoric, Barber's Grammar of Elocution, and Blake's Natural Philosophy; composition in written Essays.

In the Second Department, Ancient Geography, Blake's Natural Philosophy concluded, and the other studies of the third reviewed; N. American Arithmetic (Third Part), Barber's Grammar of Elocution, Ancient and Modern Geography, with construction of Maps, and use of the Globes, Chemistry, Watts on the Mind, Algebra,

Physiology, Critical Readings in the English Classics, Principles of Teaching, and Smellie's Philosophy of Natural History; composition in written Essays.

In the First Department, the studies of the second and third continued as exercises; Blair's Lectures on Rhetoric, Moral Philosophy, Alexander's Evidences of Christianity, Paley's Natural Theology, Arnott's Natural Philosophy, first and second volumes, Geometry, Trigonometry, Logic, Astronomy, Bigelow's Technology, History of Literature, Constitutional Law, Select parts of the English Classics, Kames' Elements of Criticism, Butler's Analogy, Mental Philosophy, Moral Philosophy, Linear Drawing, Geology, Mineralogy, Natural History, and Botany. In this department, critical attention is paid to composition, in which there are frequent exercises.

In addition to the recitations in the books above specified, the scholars in each department are exercised in Orthography, Reading, Parsing and Writing.

The Institution is designed to be useful and practical. The studies pursued, and the arrangement of the departments, are believed particularly to contribute to this end; and from the experience of many years, and from the proficiency of the great number of young ladies who have passed examination from time to time, the Trustees flatter themselves that such have been the results of the plan.

It is the design to teach the science itself, and to regard the text book as the basis of the instruction to be communicated. The students are required to give extemporaneous illustrations of every important principle in the science under consideration, and also to give a general as well as a particular analysis of the author.

The general direction of the Institution is committed to a Principal; besides, to each department there is attached a permanent teacher; and whenever the number of pupils renders it expedient, the department is divided, and a teacher appointed to each division. The teachers of Penmanship devote their time to the departments in rotation. Lectures are given in the winter terms on Chemistry and Experimental Philosophy; in the summer terms, on Botany and Geology, by the Professor of Chemistry and Natural Philosophy, and on Biblical Antiquities, by the President.

Instruction in Rhetoric and Composition, and in Sacred Music, is given by the respective Professors of these branches.

Of the present Principal, Mr. ALONZO CRITTENTON, A.M. who has had the charge of the Academy for several years, the Trustees can speak in the highest terms, both as a qualified teacher, and as a gentleman entirely devoted to the interests of the Institution, and to the advancement of the young ladies committed to his charge. They are enabled to say, with a proper estimate of the importance of the trust, that there are few who combine, in so many respects, the qualifications of an able, faithful and efficient teacher.

VISITATION.—The Board of Trustees is arranged into three committees, which in turn visit the Academy and examine the progress and deportment of the pupils, at least once in four weeks, and the result of their observations is reported at each monthly meeting of the Board.

LIBRARY, &c.—The proprietors of this Institution have for twenty years constantly endeavored to afford every facility to the youthful mind, in the pursuit of knowledge, and the Academy has been furnished with Maps, Charts, Globes, Models, a very superior Chemical and Philosophical Apparatus, and an extensive Library. It contains also cabinets of specimens for illustration in the studies of Natural History, Mineralogy, and Botany.

The increased facilities for obtaining instruction in every branch of science, furnished by means of these illustrations, are too obvious to require more than a brief notice.

The books of the Library have been selected with reference to the course of studies pursued in the Academy, as well as to general information: and while the Library is at all times open to the scholars, it is intended not only that the books shall be read by them, but that they shall afford the instructors means for opening before the minds of their pupils the whole field of knowledge. The effect of this, it is anticipated, will be to prepare them for future usefulness, and to teach them to investigate for themselves.

PERIOD OF STUDY AND PRICE OF TUITION.—The Academical year commences on the first of September, and is divided into four terms, commencing respectively on the 1st of September, 23rd of November, 15th of February, and the 8th of May.

There are two examinations in each year, one in February and one in July.

A vacation of six weeks follows the examination in July, and a vacation of one week the close of the quarter ending the first of May.

The price of Tuition in the Sixth or lowest Department, is $3 per quarter; in the Fifth, $4; in the Fourth, $5; in the Third, $6; in the Second, $7; and in the First, $8 per quarter.

An extra charge of $5 per quarter is made for the study of French or Spanish.

PREMIUMS.—At the close of the examination in February, a public annunciation of the names of young ladies who have distinguished themselves is made. At the close of the examination in July, premiums are awarded for proficiency in the various branches of study, to the pupils in the lower departments; and to those in the higher, testimonials signed by the several members of the Board. Gold medals are also given to the writers of the three best original essays; the relative merit of which is decided by a committee of gentlemen selected by the trustees; and a gold medal to the best scholar in Mathematics,—a donation having been made for this purpose by a friend of the Academy.

As the course of instruction is designed to embrace all the various branches of a complete system of female education, those who have passed through the course, and made such attainments as to justify the distinction, will receive a diploma, bearing the seal of the Institution, being the highest honor conferred.

BOARDING, &c.—The Trustees have made ample arrangements for the accommodation of pupils from a distance, in two establishments connected with the families respectively of the Principal and Professor of Chemistry. The expense incurred by a young lady, for board and tuition, including all the studies taught at the Academy, will not exceed $225 per annum. Every facility will be afforded, in these establishments, for acquiring a knowledge of Music, Drawing, or any of the ornamental branches of female education, at a moderate additional charge.

Applications for admission may be made to the Principal, at the Academy, or at his residence; or to either of the Trustees.

For more particular inquiries, reference is made to Chancellor Kent, of the city of New-York, Rev. Dr. Ludlow, Provost of the University of Pennsylvania, Rev. Dr. Ferris, New-York, who, during their residence in Albany, have successively presided over the Institution; to Benjamin F. Butler, Attorney-General of the U. S., Washington City, Hon. Jacob Sutherland, Geneva, N.Y., and J. T. Norton, Esq., Farmington, Conn., late Trustees, or to either of the Trustees.

N. B. If parents should desire it, facilities will be afforded for the instruction of their daughters in the Latin and Greek languages.

Catalogue of Gould's Classical and English Academy* (1856)

GENERAL INFORMATION

This Institution was founded in the year 1836, by the liberality of the inhabitants of Bethel, and has been in successful operation since that time. A valuable donation was subsequently bequeathed to the Institution, by the late REV. DANIEL GOULD, from whom it receives its name. In 1852, a half township of land was granted by the State, which has been carefully and successfully managed for the interests of the Institution. The income is such as to furnish an annual appropriation for apparatus, and improvements on the building. The building has recently been fitted up in a neat and commodious manner, and is situated in the village at Bethel Hill, one hundred rods from the Station of the Grand Trunk Railway.

For beauty of location, romantic scenery, purity of air and water, its entire exemption from the damp easterly winds of the seacoast, and for the moral and intelligent character of its population, it will compare favorably with any other situation in New England. Special atten-

* Catalogue of the Officers and Students of Gould's Classical and English Academy, in Bethel, Maine, 1856 (Bethel, Me., 1856), pp. 12–16.

tion is given to those fitting for College, Teaching, or the Counting Room. Facilities are furnished to young ladies, such as shall give them a thorough education in the solid and ornamental branches.

In the government and course of instruction, such methods will be employed as shall stimulate to exertion, induce habits of thorough and patient study, and expand and discipline the intellectual and moral powers. We wish it, however to be distinctly understood, that this school is not designed as a House of Reformation. The experience of many years has taught us, that where children are unwilling to comply with parental authority at home, or have contracted idle and dissolute habits, it is useless to send them here with the expectation of their making any improvement. For such we have no accommodations; while for those who have no other object in view than hard study, and an earnest desire for improvement, every thing possible will be done to render their situation pleasant and profitable.

A daily register is kept of all marked delinquencies, and forwarded to parents and guardians, at the middle and close of each term, and no student will be retained who persists in a violation of the regulations of the school. The studious and orderly scholar will here find an intelligent community always ready to encourage him in every thing praiseworthy.

It will be the constant aim of the Principal, to secure a systematic and thorough course of instruction in every department of the school. It is therefore of vital importance to the student, that he be present at the opening of the term, when the regular classes are formed. Aside from the deficiencies of his class, nothing will induce a feeling of homesickness sooner, than entering a school as a stranger, after the classes have been organized any length of time.

EXPENSES

Tuition, for Common English Branches, per
term, ... $3 50
Tuition, for Higher English Branches and Lan-
guages, per term, ... 4 00
Fifty cents per Quarter will be deducted for
those who pay by the term.
Penmanship, ... 1 00
Drawing and Painting in different styles, from
$1 50 to 3 90
Music on Piano, ... 6 00
Use of Instrument, ... 2 00

Board may be obtained in good families on reasonable
terms. Rooms may be secured in the village, by those
desirous of boarding themselves. Books and Stationery
may be had at Portland prices, at the store of Kimball &
Twitchell.

TEXT BOOKS

DEPARTMENT OF LANGUAGES

Arnold's First and Second Latin Lessons; Andrews &
Stoddard's Latin Grammar; Andrews' Latin Reader;
Arnold's Cornelius Nepos; Analysis and Arrangement of
Latin Sentences; Folsom's, or Bullion's Cicero; Arnold's
Latin Prose Composition; Exercises in Latin Synonymes;
Anthon's Sallust; Weekly Exercises in writing Latin
throughout the course; Bullion's Greek Lessons; Bullion's
Greek Grammar; Jacob's Greek Reader; Arnold's Greek
Prose Composition; Cooper's Virgil; Latin Prosody;

Greek Syntax and Prosody; Greek Testament; Livy; Horace; Pinney's French Exercises; Fasquelle's French Grammar; Le Grand Pere; Corrinne; Henriade; Racine; De Fivas' Classic French Reader; Ollendorff's Spanish Grammar; Novelas Espanolas; Don Quijote de la Mancha.

DEPARTMENT OF ENGLISH

Exercises in Orthography, Reading, Declamation and Composition; Smith's Geography, with Outline Maps; Weld and Green's Grammar; Colburn's First Lessons in Arithmetic; Greenleaf's Arithmetics; Willard's History of the United States; Rickard and Orcutt's Parsing Book; Book Keeping, by Single and Double Entry; Penmanship; Mitchell's Ancient Geography; Worcester's Elements of Ancient and Modern History; Cutter's Anatomy and Physiology; Fitch's Physical Geography; Comstock's Natural Philosophy; Silliman's Chemistry; Mineralogy and Geology, by Lectures; Brocklesby's Meteorology and Astronomy; Wood's Botany; Boyd's Rhetoric; Abercrombie and Upham's Intellectual Philosophy; Wayland's Moral Science; Paley's Natural Theology; Russell's Elocution; Shaw's History of English Literature; Smyth's Elementary, and Enlarged Algebra; Euclid; Davies' Series of Mathematics; Minifie's Geometrical Drawing.

Students have access to a large number of auxiliary books, whenever necessary for the prosecution of their studies. There is also a set of Outline Maps, Charts, and Anatomical Plates.

CABINET

The Cabinet of Minerals, Geological Specimens, Shells, and Plants, collected from different quarters of the globe, is valuable and well arranged for study. The advantages for instruction in Natural History and Practical Chemistry, it is believed, are not excelled in this State. Experiments and illustrations, and a practical application of Chemistry to Agriculture, domestic Economy and the Arts, are made at each recitation.

LIBRARY

A well selected Library of 500 volumes, belongs to the U. B. Society, to which ladies have access free from expense, and gentlemen, by the payment of an annual fee.

APPARATUS

Appropriations from the interest of a fund allotted to that purpose, will be made annually for the purchase of Apparatus. Surveying will be taught by field practice.

TERMS

The Academic year is divided into four Terms of eleven weeks. Each Term will commence on the first Tuesday in June, September, December and March, respectively, followed by a vacation of two weeks.

ANNIVERSARY WEEK

An Oration will be delivered before the U. B. Society, on Tuesday evening, May 13th, by WM. WIRT VIRGIN, Esq., of Norway.

Exhibition, on Thursday evening, May 15th.

Public Examination of the Classical Department, Friday forenoon, May 16th.

Public Examination of the English Department, in the afternoon of the same day.

There will be a social gathering of the school in the evening of Friday, May 16th.

Rules for the Regulation
of the Professors and Teachers
of the New Braunfels Academy*
(1858)

1. Each professor or teacher of the New Braunfels Academy shall enter into a written contract with the Committee of Appointments and Instruction; the appointment of each of them shall be for one session of six months; three months' notice of dissolution of the contract shall be given by one of the parties before the contract can be dissolved, and the dissolution can only take place at the close of a session. If no notice has been given of the intention of either party to dissolve the contract within the time stipulated (being three months before the close of the session) the contract entered into is to remain in force till one party gives notice of dissolution of said contract and it has been given and accepted by the other party. A professor or teacher can only be discharged during the session by a majority vote of the whole board of trustees of said Academy, if he has conducted himself

* Edgar W. Knight, ed., *A Documentary History of Education in the South Before 1860* (Chapel Hill, N.C.: The University of North Carolina Press, 1949–1953), IV, 57–59; reprinted from Edgar R. Dabney, "The Settlement of New Braunfels and History of Its Early Schools" (Unpublished master's thesis, University of Texas, 1939), pp. 121–124. The rules were first published in the minutes of the trustees of the academy.

in such a manner that the majority of the trustees considers him unworthy of said situation or if he has conducted himself in a manner that has injured the Academy, the student, or the teachers.

2. The salaries of the teachers shall be paid monthly, and they are to receive monthly from the chairman of the committee on finances of said board, or if he be absent, from the two other members of said committee, a voucher on the treasurer of said board of trustees for three-fifths of the amount of their monthly salary and the other two-fifths a due bill to be paid from the "State School Fund" which the said Academy shall receive for the current year.

3. Before a professor or teacher enters upon the discharge of his duties at said Academy, he must be made acquainted with all the rules and regulations adopted by the board of trustees for the government of the Academy as far as they relate to the obligations of the professors and teachers and their situation (relation) toward the board of trustees as well as the students and patrons of said Academy.

Whenever a new rule or regulation of any kind is adopted, or an existing one is amended, the professors or teachers have to be made acquainted with it, and the teachers have to acknowledge that they have been notified of said rule.

4. The professors or teachers have to follow the instructions of the committee on appointments and instruction of the board of trustees of said Academy. At least twice a year (before the close of each session) the professors or teachers shall meet in a body with said committee and agree with said committee upon the subjects to be taught, the schedule of lessons for the next session, the books to be used at school, the methods of

instruction, the public examination, the time of vacation, etc. If the teachers cannot agree with the committee, or feel themselves aggrieved by the instructions of said committee, they shall have the right to appeal to the board of trustees.

5. The school year is to be divided into two sessions of six months each, including the month for vacation for each session to take place at various times. No professor or teacher can be compelled to teach more than twenty-six hours per week in said Academy.

6. The professors or teachers shall be required to keep a day book (register) and to furnish annually the said committee with a tabular statement etc., required to be kept by teachers of schools according to an "Act providing for the Support of Schools" approved August 29, 1856, and to perform all other duties required of them by this or any other act in force relating to the public schools, if not contrary to the rules and regulations of the board of trustees or its committee on Appointments and Instruction.

7. For their instruction and behavior at school, the professors and teachers are responsible only to the said committee and to the board of trustees of the said Academy.

8. The professors and teachers shall take care that the students are properly dressed, and whenever a student comes to school and is not clean or is improperly dressed, the teachers shall reprove him, and after a student has been reprimanded twice and has not corrected his dress, the teacher shall notify the said Committee on instruction thereof.

9. Whenever a professor or teacher believes that a student has a contagious disease, it shall be his duty to notify said student to absent himself from classes so long

as the disease lasts, or to produce a certificate from a physician showing that he has no disease that might be communicated to other students.

10. Whenever a student is absent from school, the professor or teacher shall ascertain the cause thereof, and should a student without a reasonable excuse be absent from school, teachers shall notify the Committee on rules and regulations.

11. The professors or teachers shall cause the large boys of each class to fetch by turns the drinking-water used during school hours by their respective classes, and if they refuse to comply with the request, the teacher shall notify the committee on rules and regulations.

12. Whenever a professor or teacher notices that a student breaks a window pane or injures any property of the Academy or the property of students, he shall notify the said student to have said repairs made and should it not be done promptly, the teacher shall notify the committee on buildings.

13. Whenever the school-rooms are not properly cared for, or the furniture properly used, the teacher shall notify the committee on buildings.

14. The professors or teachers shall have full use of the library and collections of said Academy free of any charges under the regulations adopted by the Committee on library of said board of trustees of said Academy.

Regulations
for the Students and Patrons
of the New Braunfels Academy*
(1858)

1. No student shall be received at said Academy but once a year, after notice of reception has been given at least three weeks before hand through the newspapers. Children of non-residents or those who moved to New Braunfels after the day of reception and who are unable to enter the upper classes of said Academy may be received at a stipulated time if there is room enough in the classes in which they are admitted.

2. Students of parents who do not reside within the city of New Braunfels shall be required to pay One Dollar per month as a tuition fee. Students whose parents reside within the corporation, are required to pay Fifty cents per month as a tuition fee, the said amount to be paid in advance. The person where the student boards is responsible for the tuition fee. If a student attends only a part of a month, he is required to pay the tuition fee for the whole month. On the morning of the first day of each month, students are required to pay at the school house their tuition fees to the treasurer of the Academy.

* Knight, *A Documentary History of Education in the South Before 1860*, IV, 60–61; reprinted from Dabney, "The Settlement of New Braunfels and History of Its Early Schools," pp. 125–127.

Should they fail to do so, they shall be required to take or send it to the treasurer within four days. After that time the treasurer is entitled to charge ten per cent commission for collecting the tuition fees at the residence of the students.

3. Students shall be clean and properly dressed. The teacher or professor shall reprove them once. After the student has been reproved twice and has not obeyed, the teacher shall notify the Committee on Instruction of said Academy thereof, and it shall be the Committee's duty to inform the parents or guardians of said student, and if necessary, to take other measures.

4. Whenever a professor or teacher believes a student to be infected with a contagious disease, he shall notify said student thereof or report the same to the above named committee, and said student shall be required to remain from school so long as the disease lasts, or he shall be required to furnish a certificate from a physician that he has recovered from the disease.

5. Whenever a student has been absent from school, the professor or teacher shall be required to ascertain the cause thereof, and should a student without reasonable excuse absent himself frequently from school, the professors or teachers shall notify the trustees, whose duty it shall be to remonstrate with said student or his parents or guardians, and, if necessary expell him from said Academy.

6. No student shall be expelled by a resolution from the Board of Trustees.

7. All complaints against professors or teachers shall be made to the Committee on Instruction of said Board of Trustees. For their instruction or behavior at school, the professors or teachers are only accountable to said Committee on Instruction of the Board of Trustees.

8. The large boys of the class shall fetch the drinking water alternately for the classes, and if they refuse to do so, they shall be fined five cents for each time they refuse to fetch the water.

9. Whenever any student breaks a window pane or injures any property belonging to said Academy or to any student of said school, he shall be required to have it mended.

10. Students who behave well at school and are studious shall be furnished by the professors or teachers with books out of the library of said Academy for their private studies free of any charge under the regulations adopted by the Committee on Library.

6. The Altered Role

*The pressures early felt in Massachusetts to provide pub-
lic secondary education grew rapidly in other states
after the Civil War. By the 1880's, the public high
schools had surpassed the academies in the number of
pupils they enrolled, and by the turn of the century, their
influence was predominant.*

*In the face of this competition, the academies either
went out of existence or altered their form. Many educators considered the failure of the academies, and the
National Council of Education, the most important
policy-making group of the National Educational Association during the late nineteenth century, set one of its
committees to work on the subject in 1884 and 1885. The
following selection is its report.*

National Educational Association:
"The Place and Function
of the Academy"*
(1885)

1. The academy has performed an important work in the past.

2. The high school is now doing much of the work formerly done by the academy.

3. The high school, as a part of the true system of public education, should be encouraged to the fullest extent.

4. When the high school has done all it can do, there will, probably, still be room for a large and valuable work to be done by the academy.

5. This work will be largely, though not exclusively, in preparing youth for the college.

It is taken for granted that the word "academy" is to be used in this report, not in its ancient sense nor with either of its European meanings, but with the distinctive significance which it has acquired in America.

Yet the force of the word and its present use may be better discriminated by a brief reference to its earlier history.

Webster gives its origin as follows:

"A garden or grove near Athens, belonging to a person

* National Council of Education, "Report of Committee on Secondary Education," in National Educational Association, *Addresses and Proceedings, 1885,* pp. 447–455.

named *Academus,* where Plato and his followers held their philosophical conferences. Hence the school of philosophy, of which Plato was head." From this it early acquired the signification of "A place of education of high rank; a college or university."

From this meaning the gradation was easy and natural to its next usage:

"A society of men united for the promotion of arts and sciences in general, or of some particular art or science, as *The French Academy.*"

Closely allied to this use and differing but little from it, was its next meaning:

"An institution for the cultivation and promotion of the fine arts, or some branch of science, as *An Academy of Arts.*"

Returning now strongly towards the second meaning and use, given above, our fathers planted, at an early day, in the older settlements of this country, institutions of learning, which took the name of *academies,* under the following definition, as given by Webster:

"A school or seminary of learning, holding a rank between a university or college and a common school."

This is the meaning of the word, as we understand it, which is to be used in this report.

There is a sense, however, in which it would be proper to call the *National Council of Education* an "academy." This "Council" is an "association of learned men, proficients in some favorite art or science." Their gatherings are for the "Advancement of opinions and views which ripe scholarship alone could put forth." But we shall confine our discussion to the consideration of the place and function of those "schools or seminaries of learning, which hold a rank between a university or college and a common school." Such institutions obtained a foothold early in New England, and their *present* "place and function" can be determined by a consideration of two distinct points: 1. What place have they held and what was their function in the past? and 2. What changes have occurred which affect the place and function of these institutions in the new order of things?

1. *What place did they hold in the past, or, what was their function in our early history?*

It is to be noted that the early history of education in this country shows that careful attention was given first to the higher and to the secondary education, and afterwards to the elementary schools.

It is generally considered that the Boston Latin School was the beginning of educational institutions in New England, then followed the founding of Harvard College. At the opening of the eighteenth century we find not only Harvard in Massachusetts, but William and Mary's in the Virginia, and Yale in the Connecticut colony, but many good grammar schools established to fit the young men for "ye universitie."

Cotton Mather, in his famous Magnolia, tells us that "when scholars had so far profited at the grammar schools that they could read any classical author into English and readily make and speak 'true Latin,' and write it in verse, as well as in prose, and perfectly decline the paradigms of nouns and verbs in the Greek tongue, they were judged capable of admission to Harvard College."*

At Boston, Dorchester, Cambridge, New Haven, Salem, Hartford, and other places, good schools were founded, in which the young men were prepared for college, and generally these schools were called "grammar schools."

It was not till the latter half of the eighteenth century that the first academies, proper, were established and endowed.

---

* Mather's Magnolia [*sic*], Vol. II, book IV, sec. 4.

Dummer Academy was founded in 1763; Phillips Andover, in 1778; Phillips Exeter, in 1781; Leicester Academy, in 1784; and before the close of the century, many institutions, which in subsequent years played an important part in the educational uplifting of this country, were established.

At that time these institutions were much needed, and were in a short time able to perform a gigantic work. As has been said, education works downward, and not upward. It would be extremely difficult to begin in any state of society with a system of primary schools and attempt to build up from them the grammar schools, and upon them the high schools, then the academies, and finally the colleges and universities. But given the colleges as the first factor, it is easy to furnish competent instructors for academies. The graduates of the academies may then become successful teachers in the grammar grades, and so down to the lowest primary.

It is safe to say that had it not been for the direct results of the early system of academies in New England and elsewhere, the present educational status of the country would have been far below the condition it now has, and the prosperity of the nation seriously diminished. It is worthy of note, also, that the academies, in the early time, were not regarded in the light of private schools, but that in an important sense they formed a part of the system of public instruction.

In 1797 a report was made by the well-known Nathan Dane and others to the Massachusetts legislature, recommending "that no academy should be encouraged by the government unless it have a neighborhood to support it, of at least thirty to forty thousand inhabitants not already accommodated in any other manner by other academies, or by any college or school answering the purpose of an academy." Other provisions are found in this report, guarding the appropriations made by the State.

In a report made to the legislature of the same State in 1859, it is stated that the following principles were established concerning the relation of academies to the State:

They were to be regarded in many respects and to a considerable extent as *public schools, as a part of an organized system of public and universal education,* as opening the way for all the people to a higher order of instruction than the common schools can supply, and that they were to be distributed as nearly as might be, so as to accommodate the different districts or localities of the State, according to the measure of the population.

In the same report we find the statement "that no academy endowed by a town or a State is a private school. Academies are all to a certain extent public schools established as such upon a legalized basis of public policy."

In reference to the change of public sentiment since the palmy days of the old academies, especially since the modern public high school has more and more usurped its function in the new system, now so generally in vogue in the country, we desire to quote the following from the fortieth annual report of the Massachusetts Board of Education (p. 198):

Most unfortunately for the progress of popular education, some who have labored to extend the high school in view of its transcendent utility, have assumed a position of antagonism to academies, calling in question their policy, regarding their day of service as past, and advocating the substitution of high schools in their place.

We desire further to quote from this same report in reference to the province and work of these two classes of schools:

Now it is clearly beyond the proper province, as it is beyond the ability of nearly all the high schools, conducted as they are or ought to be in these days, to fit boys for 'ye universitie,' as the ancient grammar schools might do, since the standard of college education and of the preparatory schools is as much higher now than formerly as is the rank of the best high schools of our times above the elemental schools half a century ago.

Far better it is for the pupils who wish to prepare for college, and far more economical is it for the community that the academies should continue to do that work well, than that the high schools should assume to do so great a work for so few in number, while the welfare of the great majority of their pupils is neglected.

What these academies *have* done for the cause of higher education, and thus for general education, may readily be inferred from an illustration. It is a well-known fact that an eminent instructor (Dr. Samuel H. Taylor), in a little more than a quarter of a century, in a single one of these New England academies (Phillips Academy, Andover), had under his instruction about six thousand young men, of whom more than one thousand went directly from his guiding and molding hand to college. What a tremendous influence upon the cause of universal education, not to consider other forces in the community, has that one man's teaching in a single academy had. Furthermore, the entire endowment of this institution was less than one hundred thousand dollars.

Are we not justified in believing that the influence of all the academies of the country during the last one hundred years has been absolutely necessary to the development of the general spirit of education and the general intelligence which marks the American people today?

The essential difference between the high school and

the academy seems to be that the former is maintained solely and entirely by the municipality, under state control, while the latter is supported, in part at least, by a permanent endowment, and in part by a small tuition paid by the students.

In respect to the academies, "the commonwealth was to share with individuals the character of founders or legal visitors of them. They were to be distributed as nearly as might be, so as to accommodate the different districts or localities of the State according to a measure of population. In this way they were to be placed within the reach of the whole people, and their advantages secured as equally and effectively as possible for the common benefit."*

This was the scope of the academy as originally planned and sustained by the people of Massachusetts, one of the original thirteen States, and in which popular education has always had a strong hold upon the affections of the people. Now, however, the prevailing sentiment, both in Massachusetts and quite generally throughout the country, is different. The progress of the common school has been marked and rapid. The fundamental principle that "the property of the State must be taxed to educate the children of the State," now finds general acceptance in all parts of our Union. The sentiment that the "perpetuity of the republic requires intelligence and virtue in the masses," is very generally received. And since the free discussion of certain questions of common interest which have arisen since the war—especially the public interest occasioned by the problem of seven millions ignorant colored people enfranchised by constitutional amendment—the problem of the education of the masses has assumed new and more vital interest.

* Fortieth Ann. Report Mass. Board of Education, p. 209.

It has brought before the American people and before the American Congress the great question of national aid to education.

The discussion of these great topics has had the effect to enlighten public sentiment, and particularly so to shape public opinion that to-day it is practically granted by a great majority of the American people that a republican government absolutely requires an intelligent citizenship to insure its perpetuity. This is a great gain.

We have now only to discuss the means by which the problem is to be solved. We quote as follows:

> As the wealth and population of the country increased, a demand was made for a higher grade of strictly local schools in all the larger towns, and for that reason the unendowed academies generally and very properly assumed the position and functions belonging now to the modern high school, *which ought always to be supplementary to the common school system.*＊

It is devoutly to be hoped that the time is not far distant when there will be no dispute in regard to the last clause of this sentence.

We shall, then, soon have the common school system established throughout the land, including the district school, ungraded, and the town and city schools, of primary, grammar, and high-school grades.

2. The question now recurs: *What shall be the true place and the true function of the academy when such a state of things shall exist?*

We are to observe, then, that the modern growth of the country is principally *in the large towns.* Whenever the town is of sufficient population, the high school, of proper grade, and desirable excellence, will be established. But there will then continue to exist a difference

---

＊ Fortieth Ann. Rep. Mass. Board of Education, pp. 197, 8.

of views in regard to the course of study in these high schools, and there will continue to be many towns which are not large enough to support a good high school.

Add to this state of things the fact that there will always be a very large number of orphans to be sent away from home to be educated, and that very many families are so situated that the youth will be far better off at some good academy, under good influences, and remembering that these institutions are frequently located in small towns, where the price of living is low, and that the endowments of the academy also largely diminish the cost, and not forgetting that many young men of the best brain-power are solely or largely dependent upon their own resources for their support and their education; and a state of things is described in which a wise system of academies may flourish under favorable conditions.

Let us, also, consider for a moment one circumstance already alluded to, which requires further attention.

All friends of the high school have observed that much of the opposition to it, as a permanent institution, comes from the great expense often incurred in the preparation for college of a very few youth, in the smaller high schools.

A town has, perhaps, in its high school sixty or seventy pupils. It must have three teachers. These will generally comprise a man, the principal, who is a graduate of some college, and two women. The principal's salary is probably more than the sum received by both assistants. But, if the school fits for college, nearly or quite all the teaching power of the principal is expended upon the two, or three, or, possibly, four pupils who are pursuing the classical course, while the fifty-six or sixty-six are turned over to the two cheap assistants for nearly or quite all their instruction. Moreover, the character of the instruction given under these circumstances is far lower than can be obtained in our better class of academies.

Considerations like these have influenced many thoughtful men to believe that it will be found necessary for small towns to join together for the maintenance of one high school for several towns, or for the towns to support high schools for a business education, while those youth who desire to fit for college take their preparatory studies in endowed academies.

Whether this will be found in practice exactly the most desirable method of obviating the serious difficulties which now embarrass the question or not, one thing appears to be quite certain, that the people show no disposition to let the academy or any other institution or plan come between them and the most successful working of the high schools in the several large towns and cities of the country.

But is it not also tolerably clear that, taking the country as it is and as it will be, and human nature as it is and is likely to remain, it will prove absolutely impossible for all the towns, large and small, including the urban and the rural population, to maintain high schools of high grade and of the best quality in such universality as to take charge of the *whole* work of fitting for the college course the youth of the entire country, who may desire and who ought to have a collegiate education, and to do it in a satisfactory manner?

The value of the college course for any young man depends, in large degree, upon the character and the quality of the youth's preparatory training. It is a matter, therefore, of the utmost importance, not primarily that a large number of young men and women receive a college education, but that those who do go to college have the foundation for an education properly laid. With all the high schools that the country maintains to-day, it is still one of the most serious difficulties for the youth to get *properly* prepared for the college.

In the newer sections of the country, the colleges which have been established find it absolutely necessary, in too many cases, to maintain preparatory departments, in order to get their candidates properly fitted.

In most cases these colleges are willing, and, indeed, quite anxious, to dispense with their preparatory department at the earliest possible point of time. Again, in the newer States where at first view it would seem that there is no place for the academy, and, in fact, where there are none, on reflection it will be found that many of the so-called *colleges,* but lately established, are in reality but academies *named* colleges or universities; and, in many cases, would it not have been far better for the liberal friends of education, who have been, it may be, lavish with their money in establishing "colleges," so-called, to have founded and endowed liberally *good academies*. If, in the future, the time should come when a college would be more needed than an academy, the charter could be so amended and enlarged as to embrace the college curriculum.

The public schools of England, at Eton, Rugby, Harrow, Winchester, Westminster, and other places, still perform their good work of fitting young men for Oxford and Cambridge. The early academies of this country, at Andover and Exeter, and the Hopkins grammar schools at New Haven and Hartford, have not yet found their necessity or their usefulness in any wise diminished.

Whether they are to be merged into the public high school or not, and it might prove a difficult task to give a good and sufficient reason why a century hence we may not see (1) the public high school far more generally established than at the present; (2) the academy, especially for its true work of preparing young men and young women for the American college, liberally established at the East, the West, and in the South; (3) the scientific and technical schools, more or less academic in character, doing special but important work; (4) the college, well endowed and equipped in all the States; and (5) a few high-class universities and professional schools rounding out the American system of education—the public doing the principal work, and private munificence completing and perfecting it.

WILLIAM A. MOWRY,
JOHN HANCOCK,
MERRICK LYON,
D. N. CAMP.

I assent, in the main, to the statements and sentiments of the foregoing paper, but would add an expression of the hope and expectation that the free public school system may be so extended and enlarged as to supply, in a large part of the country, at least, the place that has been filled in a few of the States by academies.

E. W. COY

Theodore R. Sizer, Dean of the Graduate School of Education, Harvard University, was born in New Haven, Connecticut, in 1932. He received his B.A. from Yale University and his M.A.T. and Ph.D. from Harvard University. Dean Sizer taught in several secondary schools and served as a master teacher in the Harvard-Newton Summer School. He became Assistant Professor of Education at Harvard in 1961, the same year in which he assumed the directorship of the university's Master of Arts in Teaching program. His writings include *Master of Arts in Teaching: Harvard's First Twenty-five Years, 1936–1961* (1962) and *Secondary Schools at the Turn of the Century* (1964); he edited *The Academic Preparation of Secondary School Teachers* (1962).
